FIVE
WOMEN
PAINTERS

L

FIVE
WOMEN
PAINTERS

TERESA GRIMES
JUDITH COLLINS
&
ORIANA
BADDELEY

A CHANNEL FOUR BOOK

IN ASSOCIATION WITH
THE ARTS COUNCIL OF GREAT BRITAIN

Lennard Publishing 1989

Lennard Publishing
a division of Lennard Books Ltd
Musterlin House
Jordan Hill Road
Oxford OX2 8DP

British Library Cataloguing in Publication Data
is available for this title.

ISBN: 185291 083 6

First published 1989
© Teresa Grimes, Judith
Collins and Oriana Baddeley 1989
A Channel Four Book in association with
The Arts Council of Great Britain

Phototypeset in Garamond
by Paragraph

Cover and book design by Pocknell & Co.

Printed and bound in Great Britain by
Ebenezer Baylis & Son Limited.

Contents

Acknowledgements

7

Preface

9

Chapter One

An Introduction

by Judith Collins

11

Chapter Two

Laura Knight

By Teresa Grimes

23

Chapter Three

Nina Hamnett

by Judith Collins

57

Chapter Four

Carrington

by Teresa Grimes

83

Chapter Five

Winifred Nicholson

by Judith Collins

117

Chapter Six

Eileen Agar

by Oriana Baddeley

161

Notes

181

Select Bibliography

185

General Bibliography

187

Index

189

ACKNOWLEDGEMENTS

We would like to thank the following people for copyright permission and for their help in the production of this book: Eileen Agar for permission to reproduce her work and generous help with photographs and other material. Thanks to Catherine Carrington, the late Noel Carrington, Jane Carrington, Joanna Carrington, and Christopher Mason for their help. Works by Nina Hamnett are reproduced with the permission of Edward Booth-Clibborn, and we would like to thank him and his family, particularly Julia Booth-Clibborn and Charles Booth-Clibborn, for their kind assistance and generosity. All work by Laura Knight is reproduced by permission of the Estate of Dame Laura Knight. Work by Winifred Nicholson is reproduced by permission of the Nicholson family. We particularly thank Jake Nicholson and Andrew Nicholson for their help with obtaining transparencies and care and concern in the details of this book.

We thank the following museums, galleries and institutions who have contributed towards the reproductions in this book: Aberdeen Art Gallery & Museum; Anthony d'Offay Gallery; The Ashmolean Museum, Oxford; Atkinson Art Gallery, Southport; Birch & Conran; The British Museum, Manuscripts Department; Cartwright Hall, Bradford; The Charleston Trust; Jonathan Clark; Doncaster Museum & Art Gallery; Ferens Art Gallery, Hull; The Fine Art Society; Fry Papers, Kings College Library, Cambridge; Gavin Graham Gallery; Graves Art Gallery, Sheffield; Richard Green Gallery; Sally Hunter Fine Art; Manya Igel Fine Art; The Imperial War Museum; Kent Fine Art; Kettle's Yard Collection, Cambridge; Laing Gallery, Newcastle-upon-Tyne; Leicester Museums & Art Gallery; David Messum Fine Paintings; National Gallery of Canada, Ottawa; The National Portrait Gallery; Newport Museum & Art Gallery, Gwent; Nottingham Castle Museum; Nottinghamshire Records Office; Phillips; Portsmouth City Museum & Art Gallery; Shipley Art Gallery, Gateshead; Sotheby's; Southampton City Art Gallery; The Tate Gallery; University of Hull, University Art Collection; University of Leeds.

Many people have kindly allowed us access to photograph work or have provided information and assistance. These include: Jane Ades, Helen Beguin, John Bernasconi, Sally Brown, The Bloomsbury Workshop, Michael Chase, David Evers, Anne Goodchild, Richard Gray, James and Margaret Hepburn, Jane Hill, Sheelah Hynes, Audrey and Peter Kimber, Penelope Lee, Andrew Lambirth, Sandra Lummis, Lord and Lady Moyne, Gordon Onslow Ford, Frances Partridge, Anthony Penrose, Jerry Penrose, Mark Popham, Diana Porter, Dr George Rylands, Susan Slade, Barbie Thornton, Valerie Thornton, Ronald Vint, Angela Weight.

Permission to quote from unpublished and published writings has been kindly granted by Eileen Agar, Edward Booth-Clibborn, The Estate of Dame Laura Knight, The Nicholson family, and Frances Partridge. Thanks to Adrian Arbib for taking many of the transparencies, and to Donald Wilkinson for permission to reproduce his photographs.

I would particularly like to thank Caroline Merz for her help on the early stages of this book and support throughout; to Susanna Jaeger at Channel Four publications; to my colleagues at Paintbrush Productions, Steve Garvey and Susanna White particularly for their practical help and Ruth Pantoleon; to everyone at Lennard Publishing for their efficient and enthusiastic response especially Roderick Brown, Arabella St John Parker, and Claire Sawford; and to my sister Sarah Grimes for her wise and considered editorial advice. Thanks also to Kate Grimes, Mark Popham, and Pat Treasure for their encouragement.

During the making of the television series *Five Women Painters* there were many occasions when I found myself explaining what the series was about. On reciting the names of the five artists, a few people knew who one or two of the painters were, but most people had never heard of any of them. At the same time there was a lot of enthusiasm expressed – people seemed genuinely interested in the series and to be looking forward to discovering more about the five painters and seeing their work.

These two factors – a lack of information regarding British women artists and a desire to know more – were precisely the point of making the films; we wanted to show that a vigorous and inspiring tradition existed – a richness of images and ideas – which should be accessible to more people. A television film is a good way to show a painter's work in a very direct way and reach a wide audience. The *disadvantage* is that a programme on television goes by in a flash and once over, cannot be referred back to until it is repeated. Furthermore, there is a limit to the amount of information that can be included within a 26-minute film; some elements inevitably get condensed and abbreviated. This book is a way of extending interest in women artists and providing both more material about the painters and their work, and the issues raised by the series as a whole. We hope it will provide a lasting evaluation of five artists with a distinctive style of their own and generate more interest in the many women who have made a contribution to the visual arts in this country.

In most histories of art, women's achievements do not receive the same kind of attention given to their male contemporaries. An example of this is the difference between Winifred Nicholson's reputation and that of her husband Ben Nicholson. Ben Nicholson has been validated as an important modern British artist, Winifred Nicholson has not. Yet, in comparing their careers, she produced a body of work arguably as distinctive and experimental as his, and in many ways more fluid, vibrant and remarkable. In a parallel but contrasting instance, Laura Knight was probably the most popular and famous British artist of the 1930s and 1940s, her reputation far eclipsing that of her husband Harold Knight who was also a painter. Yet Laura Knight is barely remembered today, her reputation and unique achievements have somehow disappeared from view.

There is also something about the way that women are perceived which tends to belittle the significance of their work. Carrington, for instance, has been written about mainly in terms of her relationship with Lytton Strachey and so her reputation as a Bloomsbury *ingénue* has taken precedence over her career as a painter. A similar fate befell Nina Hamnett who is remembered mainly as a Bohemian personality – a dashing figure who broke taboos of femininity and conventional morality – but at the expense of a serious evaluation of her work, as if being a 'personality' cancelled out her strengths as an artist.

Some women painters experience a temporary burst of critical acclaim, as when Eileen Agar was 'discovered' by the Surrealists in the 1930s and her work assimilated into their movement. While Agar endorses surrealist thought and is particularly interested in its inventive powers of transforming images, she would also maintain that it is only one aspect of her work and a limitation to categorize it solely within those terms.

The five women discussed in this book are certainly not the *only* important British women artists of the first half of this century. As the Introductory chapter points out, there have been plenty of women who have produced exciting work; Vanessa Bell and Gwen John are perhaps the best known, but there was also Sylvia Gosse, Jessica Dismorr, Dod Procter, Grace Pailthorpe, Evie Hone, Mary Fedden, Winifred Knights, Mary Ashead, Frances Hodgkins, Margaret Fisher-Prout, Ethel Walker, Sheila Fell, Anne Redpath and Gladys Hynes to name only a few. And there have also been women who have produced imaginative work in all kinds of arts – sculpture, crafts, design, printing – as well as in painting. In fact the five artists in this book were never only just painters and worked in a diverse range of mediums – decorative work, domestic interiors, commercial art, book illustration, rag rugs, murals, *trompe l'œil*, china design, sculptures from 'found' objects, and collage. This is not unique to women – most artists male or female try out different techniques. It does appear, however, that women are more adventurous, more willing to go beyond the boundaries of what is conventionally considered 'high' art.

Women's place in art has recently begun to be reconsidered and rediscovered due to the work of feminist art historians and publishers. This book is in part a contribution to a history of women's lives as well as art history; here are five painters, working women whose careers have the usual contradictory juggling between work and other commitments. All painted in very different styles, exhibited their work in a diverse way and were not part of a 'group'. The reason for placing them together in a book is not to try and impose a false homogeneity on them, but to explore a range of traditions and styles in which British women artists have been involved. One important attribute they do all share however is a sense of style; they were all independent, unconventional, talented women whose life stories are as compelling and varied as the work they produced.

Teresa Grimes

INTRODUCTION

Virginia Woolf wrote that 'in, or about December 1910, human character changed.' This memorable phrase has often been wrenched out of its original context in order to offer a simple encapsulation of the profound change that occurred in Britain at the end of the first decade of the twentieth century. A new spirit of the time was emerging and people were beginning to become aware that there was such a thing as twentieth-century art as distinct from late-nineteenth-century art. Changes in contemporary social and cultural life were dramatic, all the more so for women than for men; the suffragette movement was beginning to make an impact and ideas concerning the emancipation of women were gaining currency.

At the beginning of the century modern British art was in the hands of male artists like Sargent, Whistler, Orpen, Augustus John, Wilson Steer, William Nicholson, Walter Sickert and Roger Fry. In 1907 censuses record that there were ten thousand professional artists in Great Britain, and this number doubled in the following twenty years. Women artists who were born in the 1870s and 1880s were reaching maturity in the first decade of the twentieth century and the male dominated conditions surrounding art education and exhibiting possibilities were poised to change in their favour, offering slightly better conditions.

From the 1850s onwards women artists had been able to send in work and have it accepted at the two major art establishment institutions, The Royal Society of British Artists and the Royal Academy Summer Exhibition. In 1885 the New English Art Club was founded in opposition to these two, and women were also able to exhibit there. But with the number of art students and professional artists growing annually, there was an urgent need to extend exhibiting facilities unhampered by restrictive conditions. Money would hire a private dealer's gallery so that an artist could mount a one-man show and it would also pay for a catalogue and publicity, but it was extremely rare for a woman artist to have access to such advantages. Few women painters were able to have one-man exhibitions, the name itself indicating a male milieu.

In 1908 the possibilities for women artists to exhibit their work in London in less restricted surroundings took a turn for the better. A group of male artists founded a society entitled the Allied Artists Association, which was formed along the lines of the Parisian Society of Independents. There was no selection jury and the order in which works were hung in the exhibition was decided by ballot. Each artist member of the Association paid one guinea a year and automatically had the right to send in up to five works. The Association accorded the 'same treatment to all artists, irrespective of their positions and reputations' and this meant that young women artists as well as men, newly out of art college, could show work alongside male artists who were already well-known.

Eight hundred artists enrolled as members within the first months of the Association's existence and at the first of its annual London exhibitions, held at the Royal Albert Hall, there were over 3000 exhibits. Several avant-garde women artists such as Nina Hamnett, Vanessa Bell, Jessie Etchells, Jessica Dismorr, Helen Saunders, Thérèse Lessore and Sylvia Gosse took the opportunity to show a group of their new paintings in the annual exhibitions.

It was better for women artists to get their work shown alongside male colleagues in exhibitions like the Allied Artists Association than for them to show in an all-female context, because critical reviews by men (there were no female art critics then, and even today they are very rare creatures) were likely to be more serious and less patronizing.

In the mid to late nineteenth century however, women had been forced to start their own exhibiting societies, precisely because exhibiting work was so problematic, and some of these societies lasted well into the first or later decades of the twentieth century. The Society of Women Artists was founded as early as 1855 both as an exhibiting organization and as a means of solidarity; and it still exists today. The Glasgow Society of Lady Artists was founded in 1882 (and lasted until 1970) as an equivalent to the Glasgow Art Club, which was for men only. Various women's art clubs and societies were founded in the regions, a good example being the Manchester Society of Women Painters, started by two Manchester-born painters, Annie Swynnerton and Isabel Dacre. The Women's International Arts Club was founded in 1900, originally with the title The Paris Club, probably because many British women artists at the end of the nineteenth century sent their work for exhibitions to the Paris Salon, which had a more open policy of accepting women's work than any organization of the same date in London. Male artists also had their own exhibiting ghettos, albeit on a much smaller scale. Two which lasted for a short time prior to the First World War were the Camden Town Group, founded by Walter Sickert, and the Cumberland Market Group. The painter Stanislawa de Karlowska (1876-1952), wife of the painter Robert Bevan, one of the members of the latter group, did however act as its hostess. Women were not allowed to become members of the Euston Road School of Painters, founded in 1937, but Vanessa Bell undertook some teaching there.

Possibly the most interesting private exhibiting society, certainly as far as women artists were concerned, was the Friday Club, which existed from 1905 to 1922. It was founded by Vanessa Bell (1879-1961), the daughter of Sir Leslie Stephen, the writer, and the elder sister of the novelist Virginia Woolf. Coming from an upper-middle class background, Vanessa Bell was financially independent and had been introduced into London cultural circles by her parents. As well as artistic talent she had

great organizational powers and on her father's death in 1904, she set up
a London home for her sister Virginia and her brothers Thoby and
Adrian, at 46 Gordon Square, Bloomsbury. She thus provided the
geographical location as well as the social milieu for the formation of the
so-called Bloomsbury Group, a circle of writers, artists and intellectuals
who started to meet at her home. In 1907 she married the art critic and
bon viveur Clive Bell and through him became a close friend of the
influential art critic and painter, Roger Fry, who, from 1908, began to
promote Post-Impressionist art to an English audience.

At the founding of the Friday Club in 1905, the nucleus of
members were Vanessa Bell's female painter colleagues from the Royal
Academy Schools, Margery Snowden, Mary Creighton and Sylvia
Milman, along with some male and female painter friends from the Slade
School of Fine Art. Women artists thus constituted the core of the Friday
Club membership, but Vanessa Bell was anxious for it not to appear to be
a women's exhibiting society. She invited significant male avant-garde
artists to send work to its annual exhibitions, and she organized meetings
in which critical minds, both male and female, pondered the latest artistic
questions of the day. When Fry organised the second of his two Post-
Impressionist exhibitions in 1912 (the first had been in 1910 and was
confined to the work of male foreign artists) Vanessa Bell was one of only
two British women painters to be included (the other was Jessie Etchells)
out of a total of fifty artists. Vanessa Bell was in a central position in the
London art world just prior to the First World War. When Fry founded
his decorative arts venture, the Omega Workshops, in 1913, he made
himself director and Vanessa Bell one of the two co-directors, the other
being her companion Duncan Grant.

Educational Opportunities

One of the basic premises for a career in art was a proper artistic
education. This could be achieved in one of two ways, either by
attendance at a recognized art institution with a professional qualification
gained at the completion of the course, or by paying for private tuition
from an established (male) professional artist in his own studio. London
art institutions were led by the Royal Academy Schools, founded in 1769,
and the Slade School of Fine Art founded in 1871. The Royal Academy
was founded in 1768 as 'a Society for promoting the Arts of Design' and it
was decreed that the members of the Society should be 'Painters,
Sculptors or Architects, men of fair moral characters, of high reputation
in their several professions'. An art school was also founded at the same
time and it opened its doors to students in January 1769. Women students
however were not allowed in until 1860, nearly a hundred years later, and then,

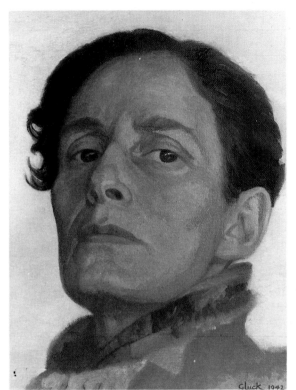

SELF-PORTRAIT BY
GLUCK
1942
—
OIL ON CANVAS
29.21×24.13cm
COURTESY OF
THE FINE ART SOCIETY

YOUNG WOMAN
HOLDING A BLACK CAT
BY GWEN JOHN
c.1914-15
—
OIL ON CANVAS
45.7×29.5cm
THE TATE GALLERY

THE DELUGE BY
WINIFRED KNIGHTS
1920

———

OIL ON CANVAS
152.4×183cm
COURTESY OF
JONATHAN CLARK

only permitted to attend life classes from 1903. In contrast, the Slade School of Fine Art was founded as a co-educational college, with mixed life classes instituted from the beginning. It had an enlightened attitude to women students and as a result many women artists were successful at the school and later achieved professional recognition.

Access to life classes, to drawing from the posed nude model, was extremely important for the thorough study of human anatomy, without which large figure paintings could not be attempted. It was this category of work that was traditionally most highly esteemed, and likely to win the artist an award from the art college, itself an important step up in a professional career in art.

Virginia Woolf, in a perceptive and witty review of her sister Vanessa Bell's paintings on exhibition in 1930, observed that some of Bell's paintings depended upon the study of the nude and remarked that

> while for many ages it has been admitted that women are naked and bring nakedness to birth, it was held, until sixty years ago that for a women to look upon nakedness with the eye of an artist, and not simply with the eye of mother, wife or mistress was corruptive of her innocence and destructive of her domesticity. Hence the extreme activity of women in philanthropy, society, religion and all pursuits requiring clothing.

In the 1890s female students began to make their mark at the Slade, and the three most famous of this decade are Ethel Walker (1861-1951), Gwen John (1876-1939) and Edna Waugh (later Lady Clarke Hall, 1879-1979), the latter in 1897 winning second prize for the Summer Composition, with her painting THE RAPE OF THE SABINE WOMEN – no doubt benefiting from her time spent drawing from the nude in the life classes. Other women artists at the Slade who achieved a measure of success were Dora Carrington, who won four prizes for Figure Painting and Composition, and Winifred Knights (1899 -1947) who won both First Prize (shared) for the Summer Composition in 1919 and Second Prize for Head Painting in 1920. Dorothy Brett was a contemporary of Carrington's and Eileen Agar was a student there at a slightly later period.

Some male art teachers looked in an enlightened manner on their newly graduated female art students and there are a handful of notable examples in the first years of the twentieth century when women began to teach art alongside or in place of male colleagues. Lucy Kemp-Welch (1869-1958) trained at the artist Hubert von Herkomer's School in Bushey; from 1907 to 1926, she took over the running of his school. Margaret Fisher Prout (1875-1963) taught the life class at Hammersmith

School of Arts and Crafts before 1914. Sylvia Gosse (1881-1968) was asked by Walter Sickert in 1909 to become Co-Principal with him of his new private school of painting and etching at 140 Hampstead Road, known as Rowlandson House. She recalled in her memoirs how proud she was of the name-board over the front door of this school, which simply read 'Sickert and Gosse'.

How to Get Ahead in the Art World

As in many professions, connections – who you know – and plenty of money were distinct advantages. With the balance weighed against women artists in the arenas of art education and exhibition possibilities, the necessity of independent means emerges as a crucial factor in the establishing of an artistic career. A private income was not just helpful, it was often decisive; most women artists who began to gain recognition at the end of the nineteenth century, and on into the twentieth, came from upper or upper-middle class backgrounds. Vanessa Bell, Sylvia Gosse, Gluck (Hannah Gluckstein) and Winifred Nicholson had access to family wealth and this definitely helped the progress of their careers.

Wealth could not of course buy talent, but certainly helped in the nurturing and sustenance of it. This was particularly important for women who, unlike many of their male counterparts, did not have a wife to keep home and family together, and were often performing that role themselves as well as trying to maintain their careers. Sylvia Gosse fervently believed that women artists should not marry, because in doing so they lost their independence and their energy for work. Carel Weight, the distinguished painter and Royal Academician, believes that women artists are faced with a difficult choice that never occurs in the life of male artists; between making art 'at the end of the day when the husband has been fed and the children put to bed', or 'going to live in a convent'.

Besides matrimony and a nunnery, there is another option for women artists which Weight does not list, and that is the choice of setting up a home with another woman. The painters Anna Hudson and Ethel Sands (1873-1962) lived and painted together, as did Evie Hone (1894-1955) and Mainie Jellett (1897-1944), the former working as a painter and stained-glass artist, while the latter was a painter and designer. Dora Carrington and Vanessa Bell chose to live with men who were homosexual – Lytton Strachey and Duncan Grant – providing yet another variation on domestic relationships. In spite of these more unconventional options, the overwhelming proportion of women artists who rose to prominence in the first half of the twentieth century were related to a male artist, being either a daughter, sister or wife. (This has been a constant factor with women artists since their emergence into the profession in the seventeenth century.) Virtually all the women artists represented in the Tate Gallery's Modern collection fall into this category. The examples which follow are only the most obvious but nevertheless deserve listing. Gwen John was the sister of Augustus John, Vanessa Bell, wife of Clive Bell (not an artist but a respected art critic); Orovida Pissarro, daughter of Lucien Pissarro; Dod Procter, wife of Ernest Procter; Laura Knight, wife of Harold Knight; Mary Adshead, wife of Stephen Bone; Laura Anning Bell, wife of Robert Anning Bell; Winifred Turner, daughter of Alfred Turner; Mary McEvoy, wife of Ambrose McEvoy; Mary Sargent Florence, sister of Frederick W. Sargent; Winifred Nicholson, wife of Ben Nicholson; Winifred Knights, wife of Thomas Monnington; Barbara Hepworth, wife of John Skeaping and then Ben Nicholson; Margaret Gere, sister of Charles Gere; Frances Richards, wife of Ceri Richards; Mary Martin, wife of Kenneth Martin; Elinor Bellingham-Smith, wife of Rodrigo Moynihan; Edna Ginesi, wife of Raymond Coxon; Margaret Fisher Prout, daughter of Mark Fisher.

Perhaps the most problematic aspect of such a list is the implied stress of the relationship; 'wife, sister, daughter' all traditionally express a subservient connection whereas the opposite could at least in theory be the case – Augustus John predicted that in time he would be known mainly as the brother of Gwen John. In fact, particularly in the instance of husband and wife artists, the prevalence of such a pattern suggests that it was a safer, potentially more democratic arrangement to marry a fellow artist than somebody who might not share an understanding of the demands of painting as *work*. Even so, in terms of equality within a domestic environment as well as professionally, this was more likely to work in favour of the husband than the wife. In the end it was a collusion of economic, social, and psychological factors that determined whether a female artist could balance traditional expectations with a successful career – determination, ambition and luck coming into play alongside financial considerations, class and social position. It is significant that of the five painters featured in this book, only one – Winifred Nicholson – was a mother as well as a painter.

The sister/daughter aspect of the list points to another important and interesting consideration; the artisanal, craft traditions inherent in the plastic arts. This tradition which stemmed from the medieval guild structure and the powerful family hierarchies of Renaissance artists, involves the handing down of knowledge and skills through successive generations. Conventionally this would be from father to son, but occasionally from father to daughter and – even more rarely – from mother to daughter (Laura Knight would be a case in point, her mother was an art teacher who wanted her youngest daughter to succeed as an artist). Obviously by the late nineteenth century such traditions and structures had become much diffused and individualized, but a pattern was still evident. Art education and state-run art schools have superseded the need for family control of aesthetic production and, to some extent, changed the class-based nature of who can become an artist.

Such considerations mark the similarities as well as the differences between the 'feminine' craft traditions; mothers have handed down needlework, embroidery, knitting, patchwork, weaving, pottery and other skills to their daughters in a wide range of cultures and societies, but these are very rarely socially sanctioned as art even though – and perhaps because – they are wedded to everyday household necessities.

Women as Patrons of the Arts

The most prominent artistic salon of the first decades of the twentieth century was that presided over by Lady Ottoline Morrell (1873-1938), half-sister to the sixth Duke of Portland and wife of the Liberal politician Philip Morrell. She lived in Bedford Square in the Bloomsbury area of London and at Garsington Manor, near Oxford, and both homes were opened to avant-garde artists and writers, such as Roger Fry, Vanessa Bell, Duncan Grant, Mark Gertler and Carrington. Lady Ottoline was one of a handful of rich, titled society women who involved themselves in the avant-garde cultural circles of London – others were Lady Ian Hamilton, the Countess of Drogheda, Sybil Lady Colefax, and Emerald, Lady Cunard. Their involvement usually consisted of purchasing paintings, and the vaguer, but equally important role of introducing artists to other 'important' people who could help further their careers, and of promoting their reputations. Patrons also provided the occasional commission to decorate a room or provide interior decorations. Lady Ian Hamilton had three rooms in her house in Hyde Park Gardens decorated by the Omega Workshops, while the Countess of Drogheda asked the Vorticist painter Wyndham Lewis to create a modern dining room. It is interesting that the patronage of these society ladies did not favour women artists, in fact the reverse is probably true. (It is perhaps salutary to compare this with the singular paucity of women Members of Parliament today at a time when the Prime Minister is female).

Patronage could come in the form of money or encouragement. Gwen John, through the good offices of her brother Augustus, received a regular allowance in return for paintings, from the wealthy American collector, John Quinn. (Though not until late in her career and after she had suffered great privations. Gwen John frequently worked as an artist's model, not a job many male artists would undertake.) Frances Hodgkins (1869-1947) entered into a contract with the Lefèvre Galleries, her dealers from 1931 until her death, which provided her with income and regular exhibitions. She was even honoured with the award of a Civil List pension in 1942, but this arrived only five years before her death.

Conditions surrounding patronage become slightly more favourable for women artists when women gallery owners and directors begin to emerge in the 1920s and 1930s. Lucy Wertheim was a pioneering and energetic owner and director, running her gallery in Burlington Gardens from 1930 until war conditions forced it to close in 1939. Although she mounted an exhibition of painted portraits of women in the public eye in 1933 entitled 'Mrs and Miss 1933', and gave solo exhibitions to a few women painters between 1934 and 1939, she basically gave her attention to her so-called 'Twenties Group', a loose grouping of British artists all in their twenties, the majority of whom were male. However, several craft galleries opened in London in the late 1920s and 1930s which gave prominence to women's work, albeit in the applied rather than the fine arts. The Three Shields gallery in Holland Street was run by Dorothy Hutton, a practising professional calligrapher, from 1922 to 1945 and it showed textiles, pottery and calligraphy. Muriel Rose ran the Little Gallery in Ellis Street from 1928 to 1939 and mounted exhibitions of the potters Katherine Pleydell Bouverie and Norah Braden, and the textile designers and makers Phyllis Barron and Dorothy Larcher. The New Handworkers Gallery in Percy Street was run by the weavers Ethel Mairet and Gwendoline Norsworthy from circa 1928 to 1931, with Ethel Mairet opening her own shop and gallery later on in East Street, Brighton, from 1939 to 1951.

Book Illustrations: Reaching a Wider Audience

One way of circumventing the difficult arena of sending art work for possible display in public exhibitions was to reach an audience by a different route, that of the printed book. Towards the end of the nineteenth century, several women artists began to gain great success as illustrators of children's books. Most notable were Kate Greenaway (1846-1901), Beatrix Potter (1866-1943) and Margaret Tarrant (1888-1959). Kate Greenaway had a head-start in her career as an illustrator, being the daughter of a wood engraver. Her father encouraged her to design Christmas cards while she was still a schoolgirl and to write stories to accompany her drawings. Her book *The Marigold Garden*, published in 1885, contains her quintessential style, with mothers and small children dressed in eighteenth-century empire dresses and mob caps. (It is a style, watered down, that can be found - perhaps rather too frequently - on gift wares for sale in National Trust shops, thus proving the strength of Greenaway's influence). Beatrix Potter also came from a family environment that encouraged artistic pursuits, her father was a noted photographer. Potter illustrated thirty books for children, the first being *The Tale of Peter Rabbit* in 1900. (Rather unusually, Potter was given a Tate Gallery exhibition in 1987, which was a huge and popular success.) Margaret Tarrant was the daughter of the artist Percy Tarrant and she established a good working relationship with the Medici Society, who published in reproduction her religious and fairy paintings, her most famous image being *All Things Wise and Wonderful*, produced in 1925.

These women book illustrators working at the turn of the century and beyond, were followed by a rich flowering of women wood engravers whose work reached a wide audience in the 1920s and 1930s. Wood engraving in the nineteenth century was a male-dominated profession, with women art students denied access to classes. They were forced to remain as amateurs in this field until the first decade of the twentieth century when Noel Rooke, an enlightened teacher of wood engraving at the Central School of Art, took on a handful of female students who wished to pursue the craft. This opened the door for women to gain access to professional training. Well-known women wood engravers include Gwen Raverat, born into the Darwin family of intellectuals who encouraged her to be independent and a free thinker. She trained as a painter and was actually self-taught in wood engraving, proving the exception to the rule that professional training in the craft was a necessary step to success in it. Another was Clare Leighton, whose family were prominent in the publishing world. Leighton was the first woman to have a collection of her wood engravings published; this book of her work came out in 1930 with an introduction by Hilaire Belloc. She also wrote *Wood engraving and Woodcuts* in the *How to Do It* series of craft books, published in 1932, and this undoubtedly widened the possibility of pursuing wood engraving at home in a private capacity for both male and female practitioners alike. Gertrude Hermes was another major woman wood engraver who emerged in the 1920s and who produced powerful book illustrations, as was Joan Hassall, daughter of the famous poster artist ('Skegness is so bracing') and illustrator John Hassall. Joan Hassall taught wood-engraving at Edinburgh College of Art from 1940-46.

The Issue of Feminine Style and Gender Imagery

Is there such a thing as a feminine style, and feminine imagery? Linda Nochlin in her essay for the pioneering exhibition *Women Artists: 1550-1950* poses these two questions and believes that the answer is in the negative on both counts. On imagery or subject matter she observes that

> in specific historical situations women artists have been
> encouraged to turn to certain areas of activity more than others; in

INTRODUCTION

nineteenth century England, for example, they were certainly directed more toward the modest realm of flower painting than the ambitious one of heroic murals. Indeed flower painting seems to have been favoured by both amateur and professional women artists from the seventeenth century down through the nineteenth and even afterwards. Usually one suspects that the reasons are quite practical and unmysterious ones, including accessibility of the subject and demand by the market. Yet even in this case it is obvious that historical and local factors play a greater role....than does the sex of the artist.

Nochlin's opinions appear to be borne out by a comparison of the imagery chosen by women artists in Britain in the first half of the twentieth century with that chosen by their male colleagues.

If flower painting was more a reserve of women artists until the end of the nineteenth century, it could not be described as such by the start of the twentieth. Artists working in France, such as Van Gogh, Cézanne, Manet and Matisse used flowers as subject matter in paintings that experimented with colour and form. They very probably chose to paint flowers for practical reasons, because they were close to hand and would therefore easily serve as non-protesting models leaving the artist free to experiment with the form of the work (also because they were colourful, beautiful, and decorative). In Britain Roger Fry, the chief proponent of the style which he christened Post-Impressionism, believed that painting should *not* be a more or less photographic record of natural appearances, or a kind of decorative illustration of literary themes.[1] Instead Fry urged British artists to paint pictures which called up an emotional timeless quality, conjured from the components of colour, mass, rhythm, volume and space, and he urged them to chose from a well-tried range of subject matter, such as still-lifes which included flowers, landscape and straightforward portraiture, with a disinterested intensity of contemplation.[2] Roger Fry, in the days before radio and television in the home, was looked upon by the British public as an amalgam of, say, Melvyn Bragg, Alec Clifton-Taylor, Arthur Negus and Sir David Attenborough. Fry was a magnetic speaker on all matters to do with art and design and their place in the social structure of the world, and he could fill the Queens Hall to overflowing whenever he lectured. His aesthetic ideals were encapsulated in a book of his essays entitled *Vision and Design*, first published in 1920 and still in print today. The names of Fry and Sickert run through this introduction and give a measure of the influence and power that they wielded in London art circles during the first decades of the twentieth century.

In November 1917 Fry had an exhibition at the Carfax Gallery in

London which consisted entirely of twenty recent paintings of flowers, an exhibition with which we know he was pleased, and which had high sales. (The market value of flower paintings is always buoyant, after all the most expensive painting in the world to date is Van Gogh's IRISES). Walter Sickert wrote an approving review of this exhibition, stating that the twenty flower paintings constituted 'serious and thoughtful work, full of feeling for the possible dignity of this branch of still-life'. It is interesting to speculate whether an exhibition of twenty flower paintings by a woman artist would have received such an accolade.

This point underlines one of the main reasons – and necessities – for this book; the difference in the way women artists get treated. The five painters in this book would not necessarily be happy with being termed a 'woman painter' in the sense that it sets them *apart* from male artists. But it is the very inequality of opportunity, encouragement, publicity, patronage, finance, critical attention and validation – all the things that confer professionalism and importance – that *has* set women artists apart from men, to their disadvantage and to the loss of British Art.

Of the five women artists covered in this book, two of them, Dora Carrington and Nina Hamnett, definitely kept within the parameters of artistic imagery that Fry defined, choosing to paint domestic, simple subjects such as still-lifes, landscapes, townscapes and portraits in a solid and sensitive manner, though both painters also made excursions into separate areas of aesthetic production. Winifred Nicholson would not have wished to follow Fry's theories, being more interested in colour above Fry's prior claims for form, but her subject matter kept mainly to the categories that he had proposed, namely flowers, still-lifes, landscapes and portraits, with intermittent excursions into the field of abstraction and imaginative compositions. Eileen Agar's work concerns itself with questions about the representation of sexual archetypes and she openly uses female imagery in a symbolic way, such as eggs and wombs. The populist subject matter of Laura Knight's work, with her love of circuses and theatres, was not of the kind that would have been sanctioned by Fry, but it certainly fell within the same categories as those chosen by Sickert for himself.

This proves two things. Firstly that women artists were producing within the context of the thematic, stylistic and formal concerns of British Art. Secondly that such women painters had an independent perspective and way of working. Both of these facts are strengths and underline the importance of taking a critical look at their work.

LAURA KNIGHT
1887-1970

'I paint Today'

Laura Knight was one of the the most celebrated and famous British artists of her day, male or female. She struggled from poverty to become a successful professional painter, and her long and prolific career, which spanned the end of the nineteenth century to the 1960s, testifies to her dedication and hard work. Of the five artists under consideration, she was the only one who became rich from her painting, and indeed the only one without private means or backing of any kind. She was a much more public artist than the other four painters in this book. Partly this was because she was herself newsworthy; her name appeared regularly in newspaper articles, she broadcast on the radio, she was made a Dame of the British Empire in 1929 and was one of the very few women invited to become a member of that bastion of the Art Establishment, the Royal Academy. She liked to dress flamboyantly, and had a confident, forthright and pithy manner which endeared her to the public as much as to the art world.

But the most important reason for her fame was her work, and what made it outstanding were the subjects she painted and the approach she chose to take. Laura Knight was unquestionably *not* a domestic painter. She was drawn to crowds, communities and performers. Ballet dancers, circuses, gypsies, boxers, hop-pickers, wartime workers, fairs, racecourses, and backstage life are her most characteristic subjects. Knight liked people on the move and she herself enjoyed the sensation of being 'on the road'. One of the reasons she became 'good copy' for journalists was that she was always doing unconventional things like travelling with circuses and living with gypsies. For many people, Laura Knight epitomized the freedom and independence of what they imagined to be an artistic way of life.

In spite of her fame, sadly, few people today under the age of about 40 are likely to have heard of Laura Knight. Although her work appears regularly on the art market and fetches very high prices, she has received little critical recognition or reassessment. Contemporary critics and art historians have either ignored her completely or written her off as old-fashioned and outmoded. The reasons for this neglect can be traced to an apologist attitude to British traditions in painting, and a reaction against the style of her work.

Laura Knight was an immensely popular painter because she painted pictures that most people could understand and identify with. But it is precisely this populism that she has been castigated for. As

LAURA KNIGHT
c.1965
—
PATRICK LITCHFIELD

recently as 1988, the organizers of a major touring Laura Knight retrospective exhibition were unable to secure a London venue, one major national gallery turning it down because her work was 'not good enough'. Underlying this response is a value judgement about the *style* of her work. Knight's *œuvre* falls outside the mainstream of modernism which has become the yardstick by which critical respectability is granted. Artists such as Eileen Agar and Winifred Nicholson came within the fold because they experimented with abstract art and surrealism, and because their work can be identified with, or placed within, a European tradition as much as a British one. Laura Knight never became part of either the bohemian art circle or the modernist movement in Britain, and refused to adapt her work to developments in modern art. By choice and inclination she was firmly entrenched in the old-fashioned, and sometimes reactionary values of the Royal Academy. But to dismiss her contribution to British art because of this, is to be blind to the vigour, boldness, and singularity of her work. Her paintings are 'old-fashioned' in the sense of using narrative traditions, but they are far from conventional.

The hallmark of Laura Knight's work – and what she prided herself on – is its realism. 'I paint what I see and I don't gild the truth', she wrote. She had a passionate interest in people and places and the way she *placed* herself with her subjects distinguished her approach. She did not just treat ballet dancers, circus performers and gypsies as subjects to be studied, but made herself part of their world in a way that enabled her paintings to convey the conviction of documentary realism. Through a naturalistic approach Knight was able to express a spirited empathy with the communities she was depicting. For though realist in style, Laura Knight's work has none of the restraint of so much British art. There is a strong romanticism in much of her painting which partly explains the cultural snobbery that has so detracted from her reputation in critical circles. As a personality and as a painter Laura Knight presented a strong, individual, and consistently independent perspective.

'Although there's not much of me, I am a stayer'

As outlined in the introductory chapter, most women artists in the early part of this century were only able to became painters if they came from upper-middle class backgrounds where private incomes enabled them to pursue their careers. Laura Knight is an exception to this, and as she described in her two autobiographies, *Oil Paint and Grease Paint* and *The Magic of a Line*, her life story has a 'from rags to riches' trajectory which dramatically illustrates her tenacity and self-reliance.

Her family were involved in the Nottingham lace trade, an industry which was subject to violent oscillations between prosperity and decline ('the constant repetition of "bad trade", "bad trade" made spare pennies fewer and fewer'[1]) and Knight's childhood was economically precarious. Her mother, Charlotte Johnson, led her three daughters to believe that their father was dead but she had in fact left her husband after an unhappy marriage. Knight grew up in a predominantly female household with her mother and two sisters, Nellie and Sis, (Laura was the youngest) as well as 'Big Grandma' and 'Little Grandma' – her grandmother and great grandmother. Her Uncle Arthur was the nominal head of the family, but the main source of income was the dwindling resourses of her grandfather's lace machine patents. During Knight's childhood, what had been a moderately prosperous middle-class family with domestic staff and a comfortable home, was reduced to living on the breadline, 'lack of money was a nightmare from which there was no waking[2]'.

Charlotte Johnson taught drawing and painting at Brincliffe School in return for her daughters' education and also undertook private classes to help supplement their income. Her mother's thwarted desire to be a painter undoubtedly helped inspire Laura Knight's motivation, 'with the milk from her breast I drew in the fire of ambition[3]'. Her mother also instilled into all her daughters the desirability of independence – not wanting them to rely on marriage for happiness – and the need to look beyond the parameters of their upbringing, '"Never be satisfied with what you can learn in an English provincial town such as Nottingham" were her oft repeated words[4]'.

Nevertheless Nottingham was an exciting city to grow up in, and Knight described it in her autobiographies as both tough and romantic. With its trade links to Europe, the lace industry was a cosmopolitan business and Knight had relations in France, where her great-aunt and uncle had a small lace factory near Lille. When she was twelve, Laura was sent to live with them, partly to relieve the financial burden on the family and partly in the expectation that if she learnt French she could later study at one of the Parisian ateliers – large studios where art students practised and learnt their craft . Knight stayed in France about a year, but while she was away her sister Nellie, who, like Sis, was learning to be a Board School teacher, died of an influenza epidemic. On Knight's return it was decided that she would start as an artisan student at Nottingham Art School. But not long after this her mother was diagnosed with cancer and given a short time to live. Laura Knight, at fourteen, had to take on all her mother's teaching commitments, the worst of which was having to instruct girls at Brincliffe who only a few years before had been her fellow students. She often worked a twelve hour day, combining teaching with her studies at the Art School.

When Knight's mother died, shortly followed by Grandma, Laura and Sis were thrown back on their own resources. The household contents were sold up and they found lodgings. Sis was not strong enough to work and Knight's meagre teaching income had to support them both, 'We had no money for clothes and had only one winter coat between us, which made it impossible to go out together in cold weather; Sis had to wait for her walk till I came back from school[5]'. They lived on bread and butter, tea, and porridge. This period in Knight's life increased her resilience, and in spite of hardships, her resolve to become an artist was unshakeable. She was finding out, however, that the Art School had its limitations. When she first started mixed classes were held, but subsequently the male and female students were separated; the men painted and drew in life classes, but the women were only allowed to make endless studies from plaster casts and statues. Although she won many prizes, Knight felt that her work was not improving and later felt that this 'lifeless' approach had seriously hampered her progress, giving a very academic feel to her painting. It also prevented her from entering for some of the travel scholarships that were available, as studies of the nude had to be submitted.

A fellow student who provided companionship and support during this time was Harold Knight. He was three years older than her and considered to be Nottingham Art School's star pupil. Laura and Harold decided to leave the college at the same time. Harold had been awarded one of the coveted travel scholarships and was about to go to Paris. Laura had also won a prize which gave her £20 a year for two years and this gave her the confidence to start up on her own. She and Sis found rooms beneath Nottingham Castle (part of the old network of Caves) which served as a studio where she began to paint commissioned portraits and employ models.

'How little do we realise the cost of a herring on our breakfast plate!': Staithes

Laura Knight's real career as a painter began when she moved to Staithes, a small fishing village on the Yorkshire coast. Her aunt came over from France for a visit and took Laura and Sis there for a holiday. Laura was immediately attracted to this dramatic place with its exciting compositions, and moved there as soon as she could. She lived at Staithes from 1895 to 1907 and in 1903 Laura and Harold Knight were married. Their marriage was certainly long and appears to have been a happy one. They always maintained independent professional careers, and Laura was always more adventurous in themes and style than Harold; his work is more classically conventional and he disapproved of her later excursions into circus and gypsy life.

Staithes was the beginning of Knight's interest in small, self-contained communities, here in an intensely vivid setting: 'It was there I found myself and what I might do. The life and place were what I had yearned for – the freedom, the austerity, the savagery, the wildness. I loved it passionately, overwhelmingly[6].' She also talks of its 'theatricality', an indication of something she was to search out in her subject matter, a deep interest in human drama – life as it is being lived by ordinary/extraordinary people. Insular communities – people bound by a shared work and way of life, be it fishermen and their wives, circus troupes, theatre and ballet companies, or gypsies – were to become her aesthetic preoccupation.

Knight made many studies of the sea, boats, fishermen, Staithes itself, and the changing light and moods of the landscape, but some of her most successful paintings from this period are of women and children. THE KNITTING LESSON, THE ELDER SISTER and DRESSING THE CHILDREN are all cottage interiors painted in the brown, beige and pale cream palette that she used predominantly at this time. Her painting style was much softer than it became later, reminiscent of the Dutch style of interior studies as well as the realist approach of the Bastien-Lepage[7] school. Faces are shaded, often slightly turned or tilted down, absorbed in whatever task is being performed. There is a strong use of surface texture of the paint to blend and highlight the shadows and natural light she is depicting.

Throughout her life Knight very frequently painted women, usually women working or performing, or preparing to perform. Some of her paintings of women are highly sensual, but in these early studies, many of mothers and children, the emphasis is on domesticity; the mood is often tender – a small, private moment, a child being taught a task for instance – but the representation is never sentimentalized. Even in MOTHER AND CHILD (1901), which shows a small child kissing its mother, the woman's hands are still engaged in the knitting she is doing, a reminder of an inescapable round of hard work and constant activity. In these paintings of the women and children of the fishing community Knight was living in, she is portraying a community within a community, just as her later studies of dressing rooms offer a specific, feminine perspective on backstage life.

MOTHER AND CHILD was the first painting that Knight had accepted by the Royal Academy (in 1903), and it marks the beginning of a recognition she needed. At that time the Royal Academy's annual exhibition was one of the few means by which artists living in the provinces could gain access firstly to critical recognition, and secondly to the notice of gallery owners. Both Laura and Harold Knight were to become Royal Academy 'regulars' and this certainly helped them to gain a foothold in the London art market. It also helps explain Knight's loyalty to the RA as an institution; it aided her progress when she was a young artist, and later offered her what was considered the distinguishing honour of becoming a member.

After several painting trips to Holland, the Knights were beginning to feel in need of a change of environment. Life at Staithes was harsh and death at sea was a common occurrence. For a long time the Knights had been living a stringent, self-contained existence, and the motivation to leave Staithes was compounded by a realization that it was important to find a sympathetic reception for their work and to seek the company of other artists. Laura Knight had been much impressed by an exhibition of work from the Newlyn School that she had seen in Nottingham, and artist friends had given her and Harold enticing accounts of this painting community in Cornwall.

Although Laura wrote that 'I doubt if during the 14 years spent at Staithes I ever painted anything that could be called a picture[8]', she acknowledged its significance in her development; it was where she 'found my own way of seeing and trying to speak of it in pencil or colour, instead of copying other people, particularly Harold[9].' Having found her style, Knight was ready to move on and discover new subjects and new challenges.

Daughters of the Sun

A painting community had been established at the village of Newlyn since 1880, but a 'second generation' of Newlyn artists had formed in the early 1900s. The aesthetic underlying their work was originally inspired by the 'plein-air' traditions of French naturalism, which looked to the working lives of peasant farmers and fishermen for subject matter. Natural light was also an important element in this approach and the Cornish climate and landscape were ideal. The formation of Stanhope Forbes' 'School of Painting' in 1899, attracted art students to Newlyn and many stayed to live and work in the area[10].

When Laura and Harold Knight arrived in 1907, they found a welcoming and sociable group of fellow painters. Many of the students attending Forbes' school had married – Dod and Ernest Procter, Ella and Charles Naper, Gertrude and Harold Harvey, Robert and Eleanor Hughes – so Harold and Laura were not unique as husband and wife artists. Dod Procter became a life-long friend of Laura's as did Alfred Munnings, who later became President of the Royal Academy. Lamorna Birch and Stanhope Forbes were considered the major painters of the Newlyn school, but there were many other interesting and individual artists. Alethea Garsin, Ruth Simpson, Gladys Hynes, and Anne Walke were among the other women artists based in Newlyn.

For Knight, the relaxed atmosphere of Newlyn was like permanent spring-time after the austerity of Staithes: 'We had never led so full a social life. All the gaiety I had missed in youth came suddenly; work had never been attacked with greater zest[11]'. Her work reflected this new sense of freedom – 'Daring grew, I would work only in my own way'[12] – and her paintings from this period are mainly large-scale, out-door studies. Particularly noticeable is her use of vivid colour which marks an important break from the muted and neutral work of the Staithes period.

At first Knight continued to paint children, but outdoors and usually as a group, rather than in the company of adults; THE BOYS, and FLYING A KITE are two examples. Her large study of girls playing on the sands at Newlyn, THE BEACH (1908) was exhibited at the Royal Academy the following year and made a considerable impact. Its sunlit romanticism and holiday atmosphere epitomize a form of English Impressionism. It has a photographic quality, like a momentary slice of life caught with the effect of sun, wind and light playing across the figures. An important aspect of Knight's work evident in THE BEACH, is an awareness of the painter just out of frame. Two young girls are in the middle of the picture and central to it; in a figuration reminiscent of her Staithes work, the older one is helping the younger as she takes a tentative step into a rockpool. But to the right, two more pairs of girls are poised, caught in the act of staring at the painter, perhaps rather self-consciously posing for their picture. If it was a documentary film, they would be 'looking at the camera', doing precisely what people are told *not* to do in order to maintain the illusion that the camera is not there. It could be said that they are playing to an unseen but acknowledged audience; Knight was beginning to explore the world of performance and to incorporate an awareness of her own role as observer, into the construction of the picture.

The Knights moved from Newlyn to the nearby cove of Lamorna where Laura had a hut built on the cliffs where she worked on her paintings. She became renowned for working outdoors, often withstanding all kinds of weather, and painting directly onto canvas. It is also a mark of her characteristic boldness that she used large canvases, P.50 often making life-size or even bigger figure paintings. MARCH MANY WEATHERS, painted in 1914, for instance, is 8ft by 9ft 9ins, and is a larger than life portrait of a local farmer Frankie Pollard and his daughter, who, like the young girls in THE BEACH, is staring straight out of the frame. An attention to fine detail in the depiction of nature and landscape, is incorporated into these large compositions. She also employed models from London and made a number of studies of the nude out of doors, frequently highlighting the effect of sunlight on flesh. (Some of these paintings, such as DAWN and THE GOLDEN GIRL, have an unrestrained

Laura Knight

TWO GIRLS ON A CLIFF
c.1917

—

OIL ON CANVAS
60×72.5cm
SOTHEBY'S
FOUNDED 1744

THE BEACH
1908

—

OIL ON CANVAS
127.7×153cm
LAING ART GALLERY
NEWCASTLE-UPON-TYNE

romanticism which today seems almost camp.) Such departures broke some of the boundaries of what was considered acceptable for a woman artist to tackle.

Four paintings that date from around 1917, feature the cliffs at Lamorna, and are among her most beautiful and radiant works. SUMMERTIME, CORNWALL, ON THE CLIFFS, TWO GIRLS ON A CLIFF, and LAMORNA COVE, all feature women sitting on the rocks with the sea behind them, the horizon with the sky forming a blended blue line near the top of the frame. In one sense, the sea is the main subject of the paintings, and the effect of sunlight on water, the patterns and swirls of the waves, and the changing hues of blue and green are rendered with virtuoso skill. Yet the women are significant in these pictures although their role is ambiguous. They are clearly not local people since they are wearing colourful, 'arty' clothes: in SUMMERTIME, CORNWALL where two women feature most prominently, the one reclining on the rocks is wearing rather masculine garb with a dashing hat and boots. They could be professional models, they could be Laura's friends (Ella Naper and Gertrude Harvey, for instance) or art students from Newlyn. The point is that we don't know who they are, they are unexplained. It is as if a question mark hangs over their presence, and their faces – turned away from us, absorbed in a book or in looking out to sea – give no clue. Their presence is deliberately enigmatic, and this, together with the solitary expanse of blue sea and dark rocks gives a haunting quality to the pictures, even though they are filled with sunlight. There is however, both in the figures themselves, and in their relationship to the landscape, a spirit of freedom – a sense of emancipation that is expressed in colour and light.

Knight's use of colour is much more saturated and vivid here than in her earlier Newlyn pictures. She has moved away from a soft, impressionistic style, to a solid and definite use of paint. This more assertive approach, is nowhere more evident than in her extraordinarily bold self-portrait of 1913, now in the National Portrait Gallery. The painting, called SELF-PORTRAIT WITH NUDE, 1913, is larger than life-size and shows Knight in the act of painting a standing nude, (who in fact was Ella Naper). Both artist and model have their backs to us, though Knight's face is in profile. Laura Knight's flair for self-dramatization is evident in the way she has chosen to depict herself in stylish hat, fichu, and red cardigan (her clothes became an important element of her public image), and in the striking and self-reflexive composition of the picture. It is both a large study of a nude, painted in a very realistic manner, and a portrait of the artist. Her presence in the picture acts as a statement of her authority and right to be there, and the dominating use of red and orange sustains this sense of visual energy; Laura Knight had *arrived*.

P.51

P.49

Fame and Fortune

In order to become better established as professional painters, Laura and Harold moved away from Cornwall in 1919 and henceforward were based in London, though for many years they returned to Lamorna for the summer months to paint. The 1920s and 1930s were a crucial period for Laura Knight in which she became established as 'the well-known painter' of ballet, circus, and gypsy life. It is difficult to pinpoint precisely when Laura Knight became a public figure, but by the late 1920s her name was appearing regularly in the newspapers, and she was frequently asked to give interviews and write celebrity pieces. Initially the impact of her large and striking paintings exhibited annually at the Royal Academy brought her to the public notice, and she also began to have regular shows at London galleries. It was her pictures of backstage life, however, that really consolidated her fame and she became for ever after associated with the 'romance' of ballet, theatre, and circuses.

Knight's fascination with theatrical life had surfaced during her visits to London when still living in Cornwall. A keen theatregoer, she was struck by the visual possibilities in the interplay between staged drama and the equally dramatic pictorial compositions in the wings and auditorium. Her early work in this genre tended to be views of the stage from front of house and were informed by an interest in, as she put it, 'the construction of it all, and the lighting effects'; how the reflection from the stage lit up 'the gilded cupids and flamboyant ornament of the boxes; the blackish richness of the plush red curtains, the shadow inside forming a background for the light flesh of women's bare necks and arms … and how the shadows from the spotlights interlaced in strange patterns on the stage boards, and the circles of light were edged with polychromatic colour.'[13]

In 1919 Knight obtained permission to work backstage at the Coliseum where Diaghilev's Ballet Russes were performing their innovative and startling productions to London audiences. Lydia Lopokova, the star ballerina, helped Knight to work with the unrestricted freedom which she required to make her sketches: 'Lopokova's quick understanding realised what was wanted. Her room should be my studio, she should never stay in any position on my account, she should go on with her make-up and dressing, stand in front of the long glass and go through positions and steps. We were both workers. There was no conversation; it was to be as if I did not exist.'[14] This documentary approach was to become increasingly important to Knight and to achieve it she became adept at assimilating herself into her chosen environment. She did not do this in a self-effacing way; her ability to become part of a group was accomplished by her friendliness, enthusiastic interest in

LOOKING IN THE GLASS
1930
—
CHARCOAL AND
COLOURED WASH
55.86×38.10cm
DAVID MESSUM
GALLERY

BANK HOLIDAY
1924
—
AQUATINT AND LINE
20.94×26.67cm
PRIVATE COLLECTION

PENZANCE FAIR
1916
—
OIL ON CANVAS
116.8×151.1cm
BY COURTESY OF
RICHARD GREEN
GALLERY

people, and the charm of her good humour. Another vital ingredient was staying power; she would spend long periods virtually living with her subject matter and this capacity to become involved in an enterprise so that she was accepted almost as one of the company, enabled her to communicate an intimate understanding of its workings.

In the 1920s her work became much looser, figure studies are no longer posed, but caught in a moment of activity – dressing, tying a shoe ribbon, putting on make-up, or a dancer in repose, waiting to go on, or slumped tired after a performance. In A DRESSING ROOM AT DRURY LANE, one dancer turns to stare insouciantly back at us; she is part of a larger scene, the casual clutter of costumes, make-up, pictures stuck haphazardly on the wall, ballet shoes heaped on the floor, testify to Knight's descriptive, illustrative powers of 'telling a story' within a painting. In *Oilpaint and Greasepaint* she describes how she stumbled on the *corps de ballet* dressing room: 'On a broken chair a sylph sits, her bare back glowing in the strong electric light, as, with hand-mirror close to her face, she tips each eyelash with a lump of black.... All is hurry and scurry.... The dressers have seen years of service in that small room; 'Duckie' and 'Dearie' come with easy familiarity to their lips – the same endearment used to the last lot that would again be used to the next and the next after them. Panto – opera – ballet – just another crowd to hook up and peel.'[15] Until then Knight had been drawing just the prima ballerinas, but she suddenly realized she had found her subject. The sense of a community in miniature; the camaraderie generated by people working together for a short, intense period; ordinary women in the busy backstage life of a big theatre; these were elements of human drama to be captured and presented in a pictorial composition.

Laura Knight's dressing room pictures are remarkably un-voyeuristic. Her many studies of half-clothed dancers dressing and undressing emphasise the unconscious grace and relaxed intimacy of women in the company of other women. The sturdy limbs and solidity of these figure studies illustrate the muscularity and strength of ballet dancers, and stress that what is being observed is *working* activity. Knight's ballet pictures are not romanticized, although there was undoubtedly a romantic aspect to her interest in ballet as a subject. The contrast between performance and the backstage work of preparation, the energy extended to create an ephemeral piece of theatre, the visual appeal of costumes, lighting, props – all contributed to a robust picture of what, for most people, seemed a glamorous, unknown world. Degas had painted the ballet and ballet-dancers before her, but Laura Knight's pictures had a more populist feel, perhaps because she communicated the immediacy and excitement of a contemporary viewpoint. Her boast/statement 'I paint Today[16]' is appropriate as a summation of one of her greatest skills –

the ability to put at the forefront of her picture – a sense of 'this happened'.

As well as Lopokova, Knight made many studies of Anna Pavlova, then at the height of her fame, and this clearly helped to make her pictures accessible and intriguing to a wider public than would normally be interested in art. (Images of the ballet came to have a particularly strong appeal for young girls when fictionalized in books such as Noel Streatfield's *Ballet Shoes).*

Laura was taken to the ballet classes held by 'maestro' dancer Cechetti, by Lydia Lopokova, and became fascinated by trying to capture movement in swiftly drawn pencil sketches. This indirectly led to a new interest in graphic arts and Knight executed a series of aquatints and etchings which have a fluid vibrancy. Two of these – BANK HOLIDAY and SOME HOLIDAY 1924 and 1925 respectively, depict the crowded, bawdy, flirtatious, and boisterous atmosphere of an evening out at the fair. Knight had painted two pictures of PENZANCE FAIR when she was still in Newlyn. Both are richly detailed paintings showing the crowds milling round the fairground and a merry-go-round in full swing. Knight succeeds in depicting the crowd as a whole, while also showing the individuals of which it is made up, and their social mix. Most of the figures are intent on the business of looking, parading, and enjoying themselves, but in the PENZANCE FAIR of 1916, Knight has included fair-workers whose more detached attitude allows them the time to stare *out* of the picture: two costermonger women survey the scene with amused nonchalance, a young girl selling oranges offers her wares, a small lad stands defiantly challenging a response. It is a small detail, but reflects Knight's increasing identification with travelling communities and their perspective.

Allez-oop!

Laura Knight was first struck by the visual potential in circus life when she went to see Bertram Mills' show at Olympia in the early 1920s, and started sketching there and at the more traditional circuses held at Islington Agricultural Hall. An introduction to Bertram Mills led to more backstage entreés, and Knight immediately embarked on a series of circus studies. In 1930, Mills joined forces with Carmo's Circus for a tour of Southern England and she decided to go on the road with them, an action which caused more publicity. 'Circus Life is So Domesticated!, Baths, Electric Light and Telephones in Your Caravan', declared the Daily Mail in an interview with Dame Laura[17]. In fact, only star performers or management could afford these luxurious caravans and as Knight was keen to maintain a sense of comradeship with all members of the circus, she chose to stay in lodgings with Joe and Ally Bert, circus workers who became close friends. (Knight later wrote the story of Joe's life as a clown into a book called *A Proper Circus Omie* which was published in 1962.)

Touring with the circus clearly appealed to Knight's sense of adventure. Circus folk were a closely united community with their own codes of behaviour and language based on Romany. In *Magic of a Line* Knight paid tribute to their integrity: 'Circus performers are not rogues and vagabonds as sometimes is thought, but a proud and disciplined people with the strictest moral code: their habits are as austere as those to be found in any monastery'.[18]

She admired the dedication and skill of the animal tamers, acrobats, trapeze artistes, bareback riders, clowns, and contortionists, and clearly earned their respect and trust in return, 'they accepted my presence in their midst – perhaps only because I also was a hard worker'.[19]

P.53   One of Knight's most experimental paintings is CHARIVARI (1928), an attempt to put all the circus acts onto one canvas. It is deliberately – and unusually for Knight – a non-naturalistic work; the people and animals are painted realistically but are crowded in the circus ring in an almost surreal way, defying perspective and space. It caused a stir when exhibited at the Royal Academy, provoking caricatures in Punch with politicians replacing the performers. The critical response to such a departure was generally negative, and Knight herself came to feel she had made a mistake in trying to be 'too clever'. This was a pity as it is an adventurous and rich painting, the visual pleasure of looking at all its detail is augmented by its strange composition. As a celebration of performance it unifies and highlights the bizarre and magical appeal of the circus.

'Painting the circus became a habit' and Knight spent several seasons on the road, once staying four months in Blackpool which she enjoyed for its robust vitality, 'an eyeful for both low-brow and high-brow[20]', as she put it. Over the years she made countless sketches of circus performers in the ring, practising their acts behind the scenes, and waiting in the wings to go on, as well as audiences entranced by the daring trapeze stunts being performed above their heads. She also painted and drew the animals of the circus: lions, zebras, horses, elephants, and performing dogs. The circus became an endless source of inspiration. Sometimes she used sketches made years before to work up into paintings, ALLEZ-OOP for instance, was painted in 1954 from a sketch made in the 1930s. Clowns seemed to hold a particular fascination for Knight and some of her most striking circus paintings feature them in full

P.54   costume but not performing, like the colourful THREE CLOWNS. This features three men standing backstage having a chat, their painted faces and extravagant costumes counterpointing the ordinariness of their pose.

The rituals, ceremonies, costumes, glitter, colour, lighting – the 'magic' of circus performance was part of her aesthetic interest – but balanced with a detailed observation of the practised skill required to create and sustain the illusion.

Circus tales feature strongly in *Oilpaint and Greasepaint* published in 1936, which became a best-seller, quickly going to four editions, and re-issued as a Penguin paperback in 1941. Its strong narrative line – Knight often slips into present tense when describing a particularly exciting event or remembered scene – established Laura Knight as a consummate storyteller in prose as well as paint. The book, together with her election to the Royal Academy, the public award of a DBE, and continuing ability to find surprising subjects to paint, made her the darling of the press and a popular public figure. Her familiar appearance with plaited 'earphone' hairstyle, large hat and cloak, helped consolidate her image. In a wartime newsreel to mark the unveiling of her famous RUBY LOFTUS SCREWING A BREECH-RING, she appears poised and confident in a smart suit, bag in one hand, cigarette in the other. She was a small woman in height but had a 'larger-than-life' personality which expressed itself in the exuberant way in which she approached her work.

P.56

Gypsy Splendour

Knight's next enthusiasm was gypsies, a logical progression since fairs and circuses were peopled with Romany travellers, many originating from East European countries. Laura started going to the races at Ascot and Epsom where it was traditional for gypsies to work the meetings dressed in beautiful hand-made clothes in bright satins and silks. After being mistaken for a bookie carrying her easel and boxes of paints, Laura began to work from a hired open topped Rolls Royce which gave her the height to set up her easel within the car and work directly onto canvas. It also impressed the gypsies whom she paid to pose for her. She painted a series of young gypsy women standing at her car door with the racecourse visible behind them, such as ROMANIES AT EPSOM, AT THE CAR DOOR, and GAUDY BEGGARS, all painted in 1938. The women are picturesque, their patterned clothes, headscarves, and jewellery making them identifiably different from the grey crowds behind them, but the crystal balls and flowers in their hands are a reminder that they have a living to make. A painting called TELL YOUR FORTUNE LADY, painted on a cold, windy day, makes the anxiety underlying this chancy enterprise more apparent. Knight's sympathies are clearly with the gypsies and she places their appeal to an unseen audience – or viewer – at the forefront of the composition. Her gypsy pictures differ from Augustus John's for instance, whose interest smacked more of a fascination with exoticism – so much so

P.55

that he painted Dorelia, his wife, for ever after as his idealized image of the beautiful, enigmatic gypsy woman. Knight's attitude to gypsies was more naively enthusiastic; she would not have considered it racist to call gypsies 'gypos', for example and was proud of the fact that she was accepted by them.

With her usual gift of establishing a friendship with her subjects, Laura Knight was invited to go to the gypsy encampment at Iver Heath. Here she worked on paintings of gypsy men and women in their own environment, often seated in front of their caravans, and executed several 'mother and baby' paintings remarkable for their unsentimental treatment.

The People's War

When the Second World War began Laura Knight was in her sixties but it did not prevent her accepting commissions from the War Artists Advisory Commission, and she painted a number of works which have come to symbolize the position of ordinary people caught up in the war effort, particularly women undertaking what were previously thought of as men's jobs. These are among her most famous images and have achieved an iconographic significance, encapsulating the everyday heroism and community spirit of people working under the stress of wartime conditions.

During the First World War, Knight was approached by Canadian War Records to paint 'Physical Training in a Camp' and was sent to Witley Camp in Surrey. The War Records expected a hearty picture of men bathing outdoors; finding the camp a depressing sea of mud, full of demoralised, homesick soldiers, Laura did not feel this was entirely appropriate. It was only when she discovered the gymnasium, and boxing champion Joe Shears that she felt she had a subject worthy of painting. Setting up her easel and paints, the gymnasium became the place where the men gravitated round her; an interest in what she was doing created a willingness to pose and she became an accepted part of *their* environment. This experience was useful in the Second World War when Knight's commissions took her to an Ordnance Factory, the Austin works at Longbridge, an RAF base, and a Balloon Site. People who sat for Knight's wartime paintings remember her friendliness and way in which she was able to put them at their ease, clearly important in establishing a naturalistic framework for her painting.

All Laura Knight's war paintings are in the Imperial War Museum in London. She undertook three official portraits of WAAFs who had won medals for bravery; TAKE OFF, a detailed study of the cockpit of an RAF bomber with the crew getting ready to depart on a mission; and IN

The Finishing Horse
– Allez Oop
c.1932
———
Sanguine, charcoal
and chalk
48.26×61.59cm
David Messum
Gallery

LAURA KNIGHT
PAINTING UNDER
CANVAS WITH CLOWNS
AND ACROBATS
c.1932

—

NOTTINGHAMSHIRE
RECORD OFFICE

LAURA KNIGHT
PAINTING FROM INSIDE
HER HIRED ROLLS-
ROYCE, DERBY DAY
1936

—

NOTTINGHAMSHIRE
RECORD OFFICE

FOR REPAIRS and A BALLOON SITE, COVENTRY which depict women working on the huge barrage balloons which were a vital part of war defence. All these paintings are about an activity, the concentration and absorption in work generated by a group endeavour are central to their composition. Even the portraits, which are inevitably more formal, delineate the specific context of a job being undertaken; ASSISTANT SECTION LEADER E HENDERSON, MM AND SERGEANT D. TURNER MM (1940) shows two highly competent women in uniform in an RAF operations room.

But it was the painting RUBY LOFTUS SCREWING A BREECH-RING that captured popular imagination as an emblem of the war effort. Ruby Loftus, like many women in wartime jobs, in a very short time had to acquire skills normally learnt over a period of years. In her case it was the highly complex engineering process of screwing the breech ring for the Bofors Gun. At 21 Ruby had accomplished what usually took at least eight years training to learn; the painting was commissioned to celebrate and publicize her achievement. Knight chose to depict Ruby in action, bent over her machine with overalls and hairnet, with the many other women in the engineering works clearly visible in the background. The machine itself is painted in meticulous and realistic detail. This documentary approach has the verisimilitude of a photograph but makes a far more powerful impact, Knight aiming for an effect of heightened realism. Knight's work has a cinematic quality and is similar to some of the progressive images of British Cinema in wartime films such as 'Millions Like Us' which introduced a new and unsentimental representation of working people.

Laura Knight's wartime work is different from that of artists such as Paul Nash and Graham Sutherland, whose tortured and surreal images represented an artistic interpretation of the angst and horror of war. Knight's images were much more concerned with the effects of the war on the homefront and the way in which ordinary people were coping with war work. Her paintings embody characteristically British values of community – people working together in a crisis – and suggest the collective popular spirit during wartime. She also documented the significant social changes which 'the people's war' wrought in the role of women, and helped to popularize a new, active image of femininity.

Just after the war ended, Laura Knight suggested to the War Office Records that she attend the major trial of Nazi war criminals about to start in Nuremberg, in order to document the event. A surprising choice for a 68-year-old woman perhaps, but typical of Knight's curiosity and desire to be present at an exciting piece of historical theatre, and her habit of extending the boundaries of what was normally considered 'artistic' material. She stayed three months in Nuremberg with a short break in the

Laura Knight

A BALLOON SITE
COVENTRY
1943
—
OIL ON CANVAS
11.6×127cm
IMPERIAL WAR
MUSEUM LONDON

middle and broadcast a talk on BBC radio about her experiences there. Extracts from a diary she kept were also used in *Magic of a Line* and give a vivid impression of the contradictions of everyday life for a visitor given luxurious hospitality in the devastated and starving city. Her large painting, THE DOCK, NUREMBERG is a daring attempt to set the sombre, bureaucratic atmosphere of the courtroom, against the bomb-shattered, nightmare city outside. The court benches with their preoccupied dramatis personae, recede into a symbolic landscape of rubble and smouldering fires. As with CHARIVARI, critics were doubtful about this change in style and reception of the painting was very mixed. But it was also a question of timing; the public were weary of depressing images of destruction. For Laura Knight too, the tide was turning and a different kind of art was coming into the ascendancy.

What happened then?

Laura Knight died in 1970 at the age of 93. She never entirely stopped working and this chapter cannot do full justice to her output. There are many aspects of her work not touched on – landscape studies, portraits, civic commissions, domestic interiors, and her theatre work being the obvious omissions. She also undertook a substantial amount of commercial work, including the design of posters for use in wartime safety campaigns and for the London Underground. In the 1930s she designed a colourful and flamboyant china set for Clarice Cliff and Wilkinson's, using a circus motif. Many people who have never heard her name, will nevertheless be familiar with her work from reproductions on book jackets, cards, and posters. For such a prolific and popular artist, it is ironic that her fame has been so eclipsed, and her unique achievements so ignored by art historians.

In the 1950s and 1960s, abstract art took precedence over representational forms and a new generation of British painters held sway. Francis Bacon, Graham Sutherland, Lucian Freud, Robert Colquhoun, Keith Vaughan, John Piper, John Minton, and Victor Pasmore were the boys to watch. Not all of these painters worked purely with abstract forms, but their work shared a sophisticated and urbane frame of reference which made the realist mode of a painter like Laura Knight seem frankly old-fashioned; she had become identified with a despised 'establishment' kind of art.

Since then, however, there has been a revival of interest in British art of an earlier period and Laura Knight has become reinstated as one of the 'British Impressionists[21]', her Newlyn work fetching high prices in the sale-rooms. Nevertheless, more than a tinge of uncertainty still hangs over her critical reputation. Knight was the hard working, professional artist par excellence. Her dedication has never been in question, but the quality of her work has. The conventional view of her *œuvre* is that her Newlyn period represents a form of artistic excellence, which was subsequently sullied by dallying with vulgar subjects such as circuses and gypsies. It is as if Laura Knight transgressed unwritten boundaries; in painting unusual and populist subjects she produced a popular form of art – a realist genre of painting – that the general public could understand and respond to. In a culture which equates art with elitist, highbrow activities, this was disturbing. Laura Knight could not be a 'good' artist as well as a popular one. Her subjects and approach were unorthodox; she was neither dispassionate nor restrained, and as a result, the world of academic art study has never quite known what to do with her.

Laura Knight was seen as an 'exceptional' woman, and she was not unaware of the contradictions involved in this perceived image, 'Even today, a female artist is considered more or less a freak, and may be undervalued or overpraised, and by sole virtue of her sex be of better press value.[22]' While Knight clearly enjoyed and courted publicity, as we have seen, it did not help in the long run to get her work taken seriously. In fact her fame was in some ways a disadvantage, her novelty value somehow precluding a serious evaluation as an artist. Her prolific output has also counted against her as if quantity was not equatable with quality, (though not in the case of a male 'genius' such as Picasso). Although she was a member of the Royal Academy, women artists' role in that establishment was marginal (until 1967 they were even disbarred from attending the annual RA banquet). Although Laura Knight, by sheer bravado, talent, and cheek, managed to place herself on a level with her male contemporaries, history has squeezed her out of the form book.

Laura Knight was completely pragmatic about her career; painting was work and you had to work very hard to achieve a measure of success. She had a hard-headed attitude to money and could be very tough and businesslike about prices. She had several confrontations with the War Artists Advisory Committee over their fees: in January 1940 she stated with asperity, 'With regard to the portraits, I should like to do a painting, but at such a price I could not afford it. The one I did of Miss Pearson for 50 guineas was in the nature of a gift; I was getting 500 guineas for such a work before the war…. If the committee were to make an offer which would not mean a dead loss, I should be pleased to paint the group, but it is impossible to do such a work for the paltry sum of 60 guineas, a work which would certainly involve much thought and time[23].'

She was the complete opposite of someone like Carrington who channelled much of her creative energies into making a home. Laura Knight was an undomestic person who 'couldn't boil an egg'. She knew that she could not have devoted her life to painting if she had had to combine work with a traditional housewife role, 'A woman can't wash up her brushes in the same water that she washes the baby's bottles[24]', and always claimed how lucky she was to be married to a fellow painter. (Harold had followed a more traditional career, mainly known as a portrait painter.) Knight believed in encouraging women away from traditional paths, in an article entitled 'Can Women Succeed As Artists?[25]', she pointed out that women required equality of opportunity before they could succeed on the same terms as men. In an introduction to a book on war pictures by British artists[26], she pointed to all the 'masculine' roles performed with dexterity by women, and asked 'If she can do what she has done in war, what may she not do in peace?' She would probably not have called herself a feminist but she painted and drew women with sympathy and insight and sensuous pleasure.

Laura Knight was not interested in politics but she was an *un*conservative person, exuberant and free, with an unconventional attitude to life; she believed that you could *do* things and she just got on and did them. She delighted in both high-brow and low-brow subjects, and although impressed by people with titles and the aristocracy, she had a democratic disregard for class barriers. She kept her DBE in a drawer with a certificate naming her as honourary president of the Brixton Wrestling Association. If she *had* carried on working in a 'Newlyn' style all her life, she would be a safer artist and associated with more classically conventional work. Her great strength that she did not; she was always ready to embrace new challenges and created her own unique and progressive aesthetic.

Women interested in British art, and British women artists, have all too few role models – Laura Knight is one of the most inspiring.

Laura Knight

SELF-PORTRAIT
1913
—
OIL ON CANVAS
152.4×127.6cm
BY COURTESY OF THE
NATIONAL PORTRAIT
GALLERY
LONDON

MARCH MANY
WEATHERS
1914

———

OIL ON CANVAS
243.84×297.18cm
PRIVATE COLLECTION

SUMMERTIME
CORNWALL
c.1917

———

OIL ON CANVAS
51×76cm
BY COURTESY OF
THE FINE ART SOCIETY

THE DRESSING ROOM

1924

—

OIL ON CANVAS

63.5×76cm

MANYA IGEL FINE ARTS

LTD

CHARIVARI OR
THE GRAND PARADE
1928

—

OIL ON CANVAS
101.6×127cm
NEWPORT MUSEUM
AND ART GALLERY,
GWENT

THREE CLOWNS
1930

—

OIL ON CANVAS
77×63.5cm
LEICESTER MUSEUMS
AND ART GALLERY

ROMANIES AT EPSOM
1938

—

OIL ON CANVAS
76×63.5cm
SOTHEBY'S

RUBY-LOFTUS
SCREWING A
BREECH-RING
1943
—
OIL ON CANVAS
86.4×111.6cm
IMPERIAL WAR
MUSEUM
LONDON

NINA HAMNETT
1890-1956

'I did not know much about anarchy but
I thought that any kind of revolt against
anything was good.'

From circa 1915 to 1928 Nina Hamnett was one of the most respected
women artists in the London avant-garde arts scene. Much of the drive
that formed her as an artist came from her rebellion against the genteel,
late Victorian social milieu of her family. Her father was an important
army officer keen on discipline and respectability. Her parents let it be
known that they wished that Nina, their eldest child, had been a boy and
were thus displeased with her because of her gender. This family
antagonism undoubtedly helped her to assess the stereotype of the
feminine and to question its limitations.

Possibly as a result of her peripatetic childhood, she loved
travelling, and acted as unofficial art ambassador between London and
Paris in the 1910s and 1920s. Nina Hamnett was audacious, rebellious, and
unconventional. She loved playing roles and was adept at adopting a
facade; hard-working bohemian artist, socialite and bon viveur,
companion of the workers; just as at home in a box at the opera in
borrowed pearls and satin dress, as in a seedy gymnasium in the East End
in the company of boxers. This ability to cross class-barriers and assert
her presence - to be accepted wherever she went regardless of her sex -
comes over in certain important aspects of her work; her interest in
people, the spareness and astringency of her style, the wit and humour of
her approach. Nina Hamnett had an extensive circle of titled and wealthy
aristocratic friends and knew everyone of note in London and Paris. Two
of her one-woman exhibitions were guaranteed and supported by Prince
Vladimir Galikine, and the Countess of Oxford and Asquith. Reviews of
her exhibitions would often cover the personalities seen at her private
views, with names like Lady Juliet Duff, Lord Berners, the Hon. Evan
Morgan, Lord Methuen, Princess Violette Murat and Lord Rothschild
peppering the text. When she lived in Paris and the South of France in the
1920s her social diary outshone that of any other British artist, either
male or female. She frequently dined out or visited the British artists
Christopher Wood, Cedric Morris and Arthur Lett-Haines, the Chilean
diplomat Tony Gandarillas, Gertrude Stein, Pablo Picasso, Jean Cocteau,
Raymond Radiguet, Ford Madox Ford, the sculptors Constantin Brancusi
and Ossip Zadkine and the musicians Satie, Auric, Poulenc and
Stravinsky. With typical aplomb she introduced the writer James Joyce to
film star Rudolph Valentino.

Nina Hamnett inhabited this social and cultural milieu with assurance and equanimity; as with most things she did, she entered into it with gusto and enjoyment. And yet there is a sense in which she was never entirely *of* it – Nina was nearly always desperately short of money and had to endure privations of a humiliating and energy-sapping nature. Much of the time she lived on the goodwill and hand-outs of her many friends. So the element of façade, of playing a role was also a necessity. She had an extraordinarily independent lifestyle with very few commitments or ties and lived in a series of temporary, rented rooms in Paris and London. This hand-to-mouth existence meant that she was always, to some extent, on the boundaries of other people's lives. Nina Hamnett successfully projected a sociable, gutsy image but she managed it, often, on a knife's edge.

Hamnett was poised circa 1915 to be a significant member of the modern movement in London, partly because of her facility in painting and drawing, and partly because of her closeness to Fry and Sickert, who together were virtually responsible for the formation of a modern movement in London. However, her fame as a personality in the art world gradually eclipsed that of her standing as a painter and draughtsman. For her two autobiographical books, she chose the titles of *Laughing Torso* and *Is She a Lady?* which stress the personal aspects of her life more than her work.

Of what does her work consist and what did she choose to paint? Her favoured subject was people, the individuals she knew in the cultural worlds of London and Paris, and characterful people that she encountered in the course of her daily life. She was a humanist, a lover of the unusual, the spontaneous, and the vital.

'I just missed Orpen'

Nina Hamnett was born at 3 Lexden Terrace, Tenby, Pembrokeshire on 14 February (St Valentine's day) 1890, the eldest child of Captain George Hamnett and his wife Mary. She had a sporadic and interrupted art school training, moving her attendance at art schools as her father's military career posting took the family from city to city. As early as 1903, when she was thirteen, she left her boarding school at Portsmouth and attended the School of Art there. Her youth and gender prevented her from fully taking part in the classes, especially the life classes, and she had to fill her time copying work by other artists.

In 1905 when she was fifteen, she attended the Dublin School of Art, where she recalled in *Laughing Torso* that she just 'missed Orpen', meaning that she recognized she had missed the opportunity of working under an artist whose main interest lay in painting figure compositions.

Nina Hamnett

PORTRAIT OF NINA
HAMNETT BY
ROGER FRY
1917
—
OIL ON CANVAS
137.16×91.44cm
THE UNIVERSITY OF
LEEDS

NINA HAMNETT IN THE
SOUTH OF FRANCE
c.1925
—
PHOTO COURTESY OF
EDWARD BOOTH-
CLIBBORN

Sir William Orpen (1878-1931) was a well-known and successful painter, friendly with Augustus John, and like John primarily a genre and portrait painter. This and other remarks made in the late 1920s about the nature of her art school experiences reveal the stress she laid, with hindsight, upon the kind of artistic training she had received and the teaching she had benefited from. It was important to Hamnett to have been well prepared in her student years, so that she was equipped to launch herself into an artistic career. After the Dublin School of Art her family moved to London. Nina's father had been disgraced – court marshalled and cashiered for alleged financial misconduct – and the family's façade of respectability and correct behaviour revealed to be a sham.

She spent a year at the Pelham School of Art, South Kensington where, in 1906, she won a silver medal for her painting of landscape. This was followed by a short period at the London School of Art under three well-known artist-teachers, Frank Brangwyn, John Swan and William Nicholson. Her father refused to pay her fees for this art school and she was reduced to performing the role of 'massière', the administrative person who arranged the models for the life classes or the still-life components. So began a habit of resourcefulness – Hamnett was always prepared to improvise – taking up opportunities wherever they arose and *making-do* with what was available.

In 1907 when she was between art schools, and still living at home with her parents, she became partly paralysed, losing the use of her hands. She perceptively attributed this to friction in the family home, with her father opposing her attempts to prepare herself for an artistic career. He poured scorn on the reproductions of etchings by Whistler she had on the walls of her room, and made it quite clear that for young female persons of her social standing 'it was quite respectable for ladies to study to become clerks in the post office[1].' She had to enlist the help of her grandmother and two sympathetic aunts in the pursuit of her career. When in 1911 she became twenty-one, her aunts and an uncle came forward with financial help (the aunts promised 2/6 a week which had to be collected in person while the uncle provided a legacy of £50) and she was able to leave the family home and gain her independence. Nina Hamnett took a rented room at 41 Grafton Street, London, the centre of a thriving artistic community where she began her painting career in earnest, with the preceding years of paternal opposition only serving to strengthen her resolve to become a professional painter.

Bloomsbury, Fry and the Omega Workshops

Her room in Grafton Street was just around the corner from Walter Sickert's studio at 15 Fitzroy Street, and Roger Fry's studio at 8 Fitzroy

Street, in the centre of the geographical section of London known as Bloomsbury. Thus Nina Hamnett was wisely and strategically placed close to the two artistic personalities who gave the lead to the London art circles in the decade 1910-20, the decade in which her career burgeoned. Because they were both well-established artistic personalities, there was a sense of amicable rivalry between these two men, and most of their followers kept strictly to one camp or the other, to Sickert or to Fry. Nina Hamnett was capable of being on good terms with both men, and she thus enjoyed a fruitful exchange of ideas about modern art from two differing but influential viewpoints. A line from her Times obituary emphasizes this special quality of hers:

> One effect of her genial personality was to reconcile differences, and she was equally popular among artists of generally hostile camps. Thus Miss Hamnett painted Sickert, and she was the subject of one of the most successful portraits by Roger Fry.

Fry had organized the two Post-Impressionist exhibitions in the winters of 1910 and 1912, which showed the British public and eager British art students like Nina Hamnett a wide range of recent European painting, work by artists like Matisse, Derain, Picasso and Rousseau. Fry's greatest admiration was reserved for the work of the painter Cézanne and he promoted him as the 'Christopher Columbus of a whole new continent of form'. Fry coined the term Post-Impressionist to group together Cézanne (who had died in 1906) and the young French painters who paid greatest attention in their pictures to the elements of colour, line, tone, form or volume, space, and rhythm, and gave these elements equal prominence with the subject matter depicted. Fry did not however advocate purely abstract painting, as he felt the pictorial elements would then be empty. He wanted the pictures to be filled with emotion and to achieve this the formal aspects should be expressed through 'the presentation of natural appearances'. By this he meant subjects like portraits, still lifes and landscapes, subjects which appealed to Nina Hamnett in that order of priority.

Nina Hamnett learnt well the aesthetic lessons Fry offered, and on a personal level they were very close in the years 1916-17 when they had an affair. But Fry equally must have learnt lessons from her, because his work during 1916-17 takes on a stringency, directness and rhythm which characterizes her work.

She painted several strong austere still lifes in the years 1915 to 1920, and then appears to have abandoned the genre, although still-life objects often crop up as accessories in her portraits. Hamnett was interested in stressing the spatial and volumetric aspects of her still-life paintings and in order to do this she created compositions that are precise and spare, with clearly defined, well modelled forms, all made from close range of tones and colours. Two impressive still lifes from this period are 'STILL LIFE NO.1' and 'DER STURM'.

P.89.90

'STILL LIFE NO.1' has only the simplest of components, a glass of milk and two books set on a surface against a grey background. Hamnett, like the Bloomsbury group of painters – Fry, Vanessa Bell, and Duncan Grant – liked to paint domestic vessels eg. cups, jugs, glasses, bottles, even saucepans, viewed from a foot or so away and from a slightly tilted perspective, so that the spectator is given the opportunity to see into the empty interior space of the object as well as to grasp the sculptural solidity of its form from the shape of its outside contour. This is true of 'DER STURM', with the two-handled cup virtually in the centre of the composition fulfilling this role. Domestic vessels such as cups, glasses and jugs were also beloved props of both the Cubist painters in Paris – Picasso and Braque – and the members of the Camden Town Group of painters in London, especially Harold Gilman. His glorification of the tea cup in his portraits of his landlady Mrs Mounter find an echo in the teacup and saucer which Hamnett places on the table in her portrait of 'THE LANDLADY'. However, all the concentration on humble domestic vessels for still-life paintings shown by Hamnett, the Bloomsbury and Camden Town painters, as well as the Cubists, ultimately stems from the influence of Cezanne. He subjected his chosen subject matter, be it a jug and apple or a person, to a process of rigorous analysis based on the geometric principles of 'cylinder and the sphere'. Hamnett's 'DER STURM' is an interesting still life, because not only does it successfully follow the ground rules set down by Cezanne, which stress the eternal and timeless nature of domestic objects, but at the same time it offers itself as a time capsule, a collection of things which express the flavour of the times. This is achieved by the inclusion, right in the foreground, of the representation of the masthead of a magazine called *Der Sturm. Der Sturm* was a radical weekly arts magazine, run by Herwath Walden and published in Berlin. It was founded in March 1910 and for a few years made itself the main advocate of the avant garde movements in art. Those artists who bought it and read it were therefore in the know, and this is a kind of sub-text of Hamnett's painting.

When Hamnett exhibited some landscapes in 1919, an anonymous reviewer (who was probably Roger Fry) noted that they were 'Remarkable by their power of penetrating beneath the appearance of things and giving the underlying structure, the esential architecture'. This is true of both 'COLLIURE and 'LANDSCAPE IN PROVENCE'. Hamnett applied the same approach to still lifes, landscapes and portraits; she sought out the essence of her subject and offered it without fuss or excessive detail, and in a forthright way.

In June 1913 Fry set up a decorative arts workshop, called the Omega Workshops, at 33 Fitzroy Square, Bloomsbury. He established Omega for two main reasons: to offer patronage for the younger artists in London who had expressed interest in his two Post-Impressionist exhibitions and wished to work in a similar manner, and to offer the opportunity for these same artists to apply Post-Impressionist principles to objects of domestic use, rather than to paintings. Fry realized that while the British public were unlikely to buy Post-Impressionist paintings, they might be persuaded to buy curtains, trays, tables and crockery, and so on, decorated in the most modern artistic style. Fry's offer of patronage amounted to a wage of thirty shillings a week for all artists employed at the Omega, and since Fry's daughter recalled that at this time they paid their gardener one guinea a week, this amount was a low but adequate weekly wage.

Nina Hamnett recorded that 'feeling brave one morning I went to Fitzroy Square and asked to see Mr Fry[2].' He took her on as an Omega employee immediately and for the first couple of years of the Omega's existence Hamnett undertook small-scale tasks such as painting free-hand colourful decorations onto wooden candlesticks. She was also responsible for introducing the sculptor Henri Gaudier-Brzeska and the painter Roald Kristian (her husband) to Fry and to the offer of paid employment at the Omega. There were three artist-directors of the Omega Workshops – Fry himself, and Duncan Grant and Vanessa Bell. Vanessa Bell's influence upon Fry was strong during the years 1913-15, at a time when they were still deeply involved with one another, following an affair they had had in 1911. However, Vanessa Bell severed her ties with the Omega in 1916, and this gave room for Hamnett to come into the foreground, both as an Omega Workshops artist and as a central figure in Fry's life. Fry would have admired and possibly made use of Hamnett's first-hand knowledge of modern French art, gained from her regular visits to Paris and her acquaintance with the leaders of the avant-garde circles there. In the autumn of 1916 Fry employed Hamnett to work with him on an important mural commission for the flat of Arthur Ruck at 4 Berkeley Street, London (the mural decorations are no longer extant) and began a series of portraits of her, posing both clothed and naked. He also immortalized her as a languid reclining nude (her short haircut with its distinctive fringe helps to identify her as the model) on a painted Omega Workshops bedhead.

She had learnt to be proud of her lithe body from the time when, against her family's moral principles, she had examined herself naked in her mirror and used what she saw as an extension to the life classes at art school, drawing from her reflection with independent pride. Hamnett's subsequent presentation of herself as a free, adventurous and untrammelled spirit was formed in opposition to her prudish and constrained upbringing. She was not, therefore, inhibited about posing naked for Fry. Some of Hamnet's ink drawings of a male nude from this period resemble Fry and it is quite probable that he also posed naked for her. But although he would have countenanced the idea of exhibiting paintings or drawings of Nina Hamnett that showed her naked, the reverse scenario would have been unlikely. The presentation of the male nude by a female artist is still, in the last decades of the twentieth century, a concept that appears to be breaking some unspoken artistic and cultural rules.

The thirty shilling weekly wage from the Omega Workshops was one form of paid employment that came Hamnett's way. She had another part-time job teaching drawing at the Westminster Technical Institute for two terms in the winter of 1919, a job which she was given on the recommendation of Walter Sickert. But the Omega wage ceased when the workshops closed in July 1919, and Nina resigned from her post at the Westminster Institute in favour of life and work in Paris. Her bravery – and perhaps foolhardiness – in throwing up this job and its attendant salary illustrates the part of her character that drove her on and contributed to a sense of survival whatever the odds. Winifred Gill, a fellow employee at the Omega, met up with Hamnett much later in the early 1950s and suggested that she apply for some false teeth (she was lacking her front top teeth) on the National Health Service. Nina Hamnett adamantly refused such help fearing that her application would cause her to become registered on official lists. Nina Hamnett was always fiercely independent and though willing to borrow or beg from her friends, would not break certain unwritten rules, one of which was a hatred of 'bourgeois' petty officialdom and a determination to 'have no truck' with it.

'She draws like a born sculptor'
(Sickert 1918)

When Osbert Sitwell's book *The People's Album of London Statues* with her witty and highly praised line illustrations was published in 1928, Nina Hamnett was interviewed by a journalist from the *Birmingham Evening Despatch*, who was anxious to point up her connections with his city. The article was entitled 'Birmingham Artist's Drawings[3]' and it began by telling readers that Nina was the daughter of the late Captain George Edward Hamnett, a member of a well-known Birmingham family, with a distinguished military record. It was also said that her grandfather was the late Captain Edwin Archdeacon who charted with his own hand the

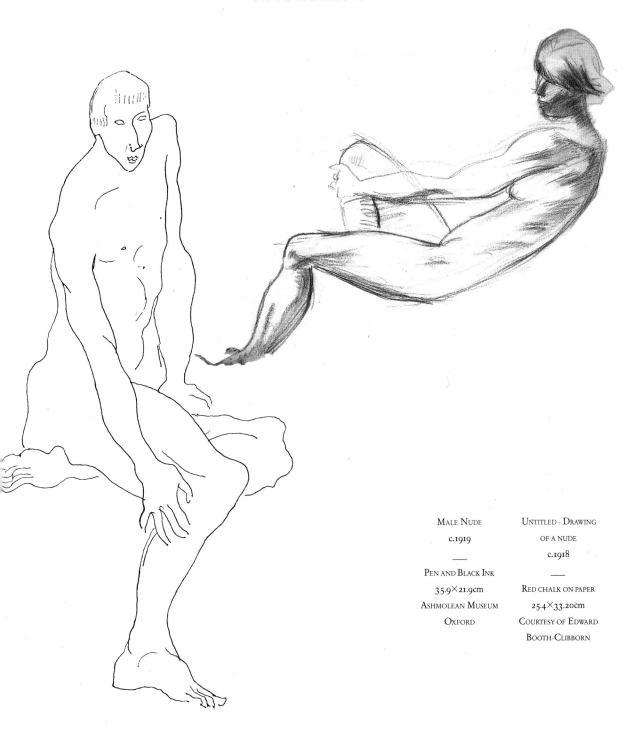

MALE NUDE
c.1919

—

PEN AND BLACK INK
35.9×21.9cm
ASHMOLEAN MUSEUM
OXFORD

UNTITLED - DRAWING
OF A NUDE
c.1918

—

RED CHALK ON PAPER
25.4×33.20cm
COURTESY OF EDWARD
BOOTH-CLIBBORN

coastline of Wales, and the seaboard of Western Australia. From this starting point Hamnett announced: 'I suppose that my art to a great extent is inherited from my family.' Since this could not in any way refer to her father, she must have meant that the cartographic and draughtsman's skills of her maternal grandfather were of influence in the development of her own fluent line drawings.

Walter Sickert wrote the preface for her first solo exhibition of paintings and drawings at the Eldar Gallery, Great Marlborough Street, London in June 1918 (this itself was a great honour for a young woman artist) and was highly enthusiastic about her paintings and drawings. He wrote about each category separately, although noting that to be a complete artist one needed to both paint and draw well:

> Nina Hamnett had the luck to be born with the two
> complementary gifts that are needed for the equipment of the
> complete artist. She draws like a born sculptor and paints like a
> born painter. Either gift is rare, and the chances against the
> coincidence are enormous. She has farmed both estates sedulously
> and separately ... and she has had, or rather made for herself, some
> marvellous opportunities ... To have drawn constantly from the
> figure by the side of such sculptors as Gaudier-Brzeska and
> Modigliani does not fall to the lot of most young students.

Hamnett met the sculptor Henri Gaudier-Brzeska (1891-1915) in the summer of 1913 after they had both sent work into the Allied Artists' Association exhibition at the Albert Hall in June 1913, and registered a strong interest in each others' work. Gaudier-Brzeska shared a similar outlook on life to Hamnett and was prepared to suffer financial and domestic hardships in order to pursue an independent career as an artist. After his premature death in the First World War, Ezra Pound described Gaudier-Brzeska as 'a wolf in the woods without a collar', this emotive and poetic phrase encapsulating the way Gaudier-Brzeska lived life at a furious pace with a complete disregard for conventions; this also characterizes Hamnett.

Henri Gaudier had arrived in London from Paris in 1911, believing London rather than Paris to be the lively centre of the avant-garde art world, in the company of a strange nervous Polish woman twenty years his senior whose name was Sophie Brzeska. She believed in Gaudier's artistic talents and was prepared to support him both domestically and morally, although poverty and a horror of social occasions hampered her assistance in these directions. In order to indicate their solidarity with each other, they took each other's surname.

Gaudier-Brzeska was a highly articulate young man who had taken every opportunity while in Paris to learn what constituted the cutting-edge of modern art. He knew about Post-Impressionism and Cubism and was aware that directness of expression, strength and sureness of form with an avoidance of detail was what the modern movement in art was founded upon. By 1913 when he met Nina Hamnett he had pared down his drawing style from a cubistic one with angular hatched areas of shadow into a most economical statement of a pure flowing pen line. He is popularly famous for this drawing style, and it is similar to the style in which Nina Hamnett excelled. She accompanied Gaudier-Brzeska to an evening sketching class in Chelsea and they drew from the nude figure side by side - see MALE NUDE. It is not possible to identify influences from either Gaudier to Hamnett or the other way round because both arrived at their consummate pen line drawing style at the same time. It was perhaps less a question of influence and more a question of supporting one another in order to forge a path forward through the thickets of the art world . Hamnett also, at Gaudier-Brzeska's request, posed nude for him as a model and for all her independence fell into the standard role model that a woman with a handsome and available body provides for a dominant male artist colleague. Sophie Brzeska, not being an artist, was jealous of the time that Nina and Henri spent together and surmised that they had an affair. To give Gaudier credit however, Hamnett recalled in *Laughing Torso* how, after drawing from her nude body, Gaudier took off his own clothes and struck a pose for her[4].

In 1913 Gaudier carved a small white marble torso using Hamnett as a model, and it was this work and this experience which provided her with the title of her first volume of autobiography, *Laughing Torso*. After his death Hamnett gave away some of Gaudier-Brzeska's drawings so as to make his name and his art more widely known and appreciated. Osbert Sitwell, a friend, admirer and sitter to Nina Hamnett, wrote of her in 1942 that 'Generosity ... is so marked a feature in her character that she longs to introduce her friends one to another, to make presents of them, as it were, in the same way in which she gave away drawings by Modigliani and Gaudier-Brzeska...[5]'.

Nina Hamnett's close friendship with Gaudier-Brzeska, combined with a short visit to Paris in 1912, had made her all the more eager to enter into the art world coteries of Paris. A gift of £30 from a wealthy female friend provided the means while Nina Hamnett's own brave spirit of adventure provided the momentum. With only a smattering of schoolgirl French and the address of a cheap restaurant given her by the sculptor Jacob Epstein (whom she had met through Augustus John) she took the cross-channel steamer sometime in the spring of 1914. She sat alone in this restaurant on her first evening in Paris and even before beginning her dinner was accosted by the artist Amedeo Modigliani, who had come into the restaurant in order to attempt to sell some of his drawings. Because

Modigliani was at this time making sculpture rather than paintings, his drawings, like those of Henri Gaudier-Brzeska, concentrated on a strong telling contour and were devoid of detail. Hamnett immediately bought a pencil drawing of a head and recalled, 'Whenever I had any money to spare I would buy one of his drawings.... He used to drink a great deal of wine, and absinthe when he could afford it. Picasso and the really good artists thought him very talented and bought his works, but the majority of the people in the Quarter thought of him only as a perfect nuisance and told me that I was wasting my money[6]'. When she wrote this in her autobiography she underplayed the fact that she too, like Picasso, was one of the first to recognize Modigliani's talents when others derided him.

It is fitting that the description of her talents and œuvre in her *Times* obituary began 'sculptress, painter and authoress'; although she is never credited with a single piece of three-dimensional work in her whole career, this very close comradeship with two of the most avant-garde sculptors in early twentieth century modern art, Gaudier-Brzeska and Modigliani, had given rise to the idea that she too had matched them in her appreciation of sculptural form. Hamnett's work, in particular her drawings (see figs), have a very sculptural feel; with an assured few lines she was able to convey a strong sense of form.

Hamnett made quite an impression in Paris with her brightly coloured Omega clothes, and she clearly enjoyed dressing for effect; 'I had a wonderful collection of stockings at that time and wore flat-heeled shoes with straps on them like children do. They made my feet look very large. They cost five francs and were worn by concierges. I had red stockings and yellow stockings and some that looked like a chess board. Modigliani would run up after me up the Boulevard Raspail after the Rotonde had closed. He could always see me because of my loud stockings.'[7]

In 1914, after falling in love with him from afar across the tables of a Paris café, she paid for a penniless but talented Norwegian artist three years her junior called Roald Kristian, (whom she refers to in *Laughing Torso* as Edgar de Bergen) to travel from Paris and live with her in London. She married him at a Brentford registry office on 12th October 1914 but soon realized that it had been an error of judgement on her part, partly because of the incompatibility of their personalities and partly because she felt restricted by the conventional expectations of married life. By this time she was pregnant, and a son born of this strange marriage died soon after birth in March 1915. Nina Hamnett lost touch with Roald Kristian after 1917 when he was arrested as an enemy alien and deported to France to fight for the Belgian army. She never divorced him however, thus remaining officially married all her life (as Kristian was a

Nina Hamnett

foreigner, Hamnett lost some of her civil rights by this marriage, but Kristian's disappearance plus the bureacracy and *cost* of divorce proceedings prevented her regaining single status). Hamnett had a later, long-term relationship with a Polish artist Waclow Zawadowski (known as 'Zawado'), with whom she lived in Paris. She however, professed to be unsuited to monogamy and preferred a more independent existence, 'I found it much better to live by myself and to have no one to wait for one's arrival home'[8].

'She is chiefly interested in Man'

Walter Sickert was a painter of figures and urban scenes who spent a short time as an actor early on in his career. This love of the stage and the playing of roles never left him and his art reflected the actor's role of being an interpreter of human actions and feelings. Since childhood, Hamnett had also cherished an ambition to go on the stage and for two short weeks in 1910 she appeared in the chorus of a musical called 'Proud Maisie' at the Aldwych Theatre, London. Although this constituted the full extent of her acting career, the notion of being a performer, never left her. Performing satisfied the audacious, exhibitionist side of her character and she was famous for singing lively, sometimes bawdy, songs to her own guitar accompaniment, for her extensive knowledge of rude limericks, and as she recounts in *Laughing Torso*, she had been known to abandon her clothes and dance naked at parties. There were undoubtedly periods in Hamnett's life when the performer in her took the upper hand to the detriment of her painting career. She knew that she needed to find a balance between the dual sides of her personality – the witty entertainer and the serious dedicated painter – but wasn't always able to achieve her good resolutions. In the 1930s and 1940s the social side of Nina Hamnett's life overwhelmed her work. But the role of performer was also intertwined with her aesthetic interest. Like Sickert, Hamnett was an acute observer of mankind; such observation being one of the

P.91 prerequisites of acting, helping to provide the performer with his or her material. Whatever struck Hamnett as interesting or amusing, or striking in a person's physiognomy or in a group of people, she would note down quickly and deftly in small pen or pencil sketches. Her family possess an illustrated diary which she kept while in hospital during the years 1954-6 and amongst her writings are stuck tiny drawings, some no bigger than two inches square, of fellow sufferers, captured in moments of sleep or relaxation. Hamnett was always a realist and had a kind of brusque honesty; she was never in the least bit sentimental. In 1927 the young writer Basil Bunting provided a profile of the life and work of Nina Hamnett for a series in *The Outlook* magazine entitled 'Some of our

Contemporaries'. In this complimentary profile he wrote:

> Nina Hamnett is one of those very rare painters who really see life
> and art for themselves instead of being content to think in the
> terms that have been made familiar by fashion, the art schools and
> the Masters.... Her talent is robustly English ... a writer in *The
> Times* has recently compared her to Cruikshank. Like him she is
> chiefly interested in Man; Man in his clothes and civilised and
> living among crowds, in public houses, restaurants, streets and
> tramcars.... But the sureness of her consummate line relates her
> more directly to Daumier or Rowlandson[9].

Her line drawings and watercolours of figures certainly connect
her to a graphic tradition in English art, and her humour is particularly
P.94   evident in this genre. It was also a way of exploring areas of English life –
pub, music hall, boxing ring, park bench, market stall – and expressing
her interest in urban social pleasures and entertainment.

Spirit of the Age

Nina Hamnett's oil portraits reveal her work at its most
impressive. But because – as a body of work – her portraits have been
dispersed, not well illustrated or critically reviewed in recent decades,
they have been unjustly overlooked. Her career in portraiture has a
cyclical nature; the first work she ever exhibited in public was a
watercolour study of a child, shown at the Walker Art Gallery, Liverpool
in the autumn of 1911, and the last concentrated group of works she
executed in 1953-4 were red chalk drawings of young boys lost in
concentration while reading or playing. From July 1913 when she began
every few months to send her work to avant-garde London exhibitions,
her subject was exclusively portraiture. Still lifes and townscapes begin to
make an appearance in her work in 1916, but these subjects remain quite
outnumbered by portraits.

In 1924 Nina Hamnett was reported as saying 'My ambition is to
paint psychological portraits that shall represent accurately the spirit of
the age[10].' There are several major portraits which testify to the fulfilment
of that ambition. Since she knew almost everyone of note in the cultural
and social worlds of London and Paris during the 1910s to 1930s, she
painted and drew a high proportion of well-known characters, including
Walter Sickert, Edith and Osbert Sitwell, Ossip Zadkine, Amedeo
Modigliani, Frank Dobson, Henri Gaudier-Brzeska, Francis Poulenc,
Georges Auric, Rupert Doone, W.H.Davies, Anthony Powell, Roger Fry
and Lytton Strachey. Her portraits are an encapsulation of the spirit of
that age forcefully reminding us of the social milieu in which she lived and

P.92,93 worked and the sensitivity with which she recorded her outlook on the contemporary scene. Her portraits of RUPERT DOONE and JAMES HEPBURN are stylized, witty characterizations with the elongated heads reminiscent of Modigliani's work. Rupert Doone was a ballet dancer and Hamnett was immediately struck by his aesthetic good looks, but could not afford to pay him to sit for her. Nevertheless, with characteristic resourcefulness she got him a job posing at an Academy of Art where she could work at her portrait. James Hepburn is the son of the poet Anna Wickham, a long-standing friend of Hamnett's and he and his brother John performed as a cabaret and music hall act. These soigné young men succinctly convey the atmosphere of Parisian cafe society of the 1920's in which Nina Hamnett played her part with so much zest.

Hamnett was gifted with the capacity to grasp the essential in both the form and the character of her sitters and to set this down with subtlety and strength. This was helped by her use of a subdued yet quietly rich range of colours, in which she could well have been encouraged by both Sickert and Fry. When Sickert enticed her to follow him to Bath in 1918, she painted the portrait of her landlady there:

> the widow of a policeman. She wore a striped blue and white blouse with a belt, a large cameo brooch, and her hair in a bun.... I did a life-sized painting of her with family photographs in suitable frames on the table and a telescope[11].

A letter from Hamnett to Sickert reveals that the landlady's son was a sailor and the large telescope on the table was his. The widowed landlady sits resolutely alone in her room, with a teacup and her son's telescope on the table before her, her hand resting beside these objects. The telescope is not only included in the composition as a strong horizontal form which adds emphasis to the lower half of the picture, but it is also there to add psychological weight. Nina Hamnett has managed, by this object, to indicate something about the maternal concerns of her landlady, her pride in her son and concern for his welfare. Van Gogh painted a similarly charged portrait, WOMAN ROCKING A CRADLE, a portrait of Madame Rolin, seated like Nina Hamnett's landlady in front of heavily patterned wallpaper and holding in her hand a length of rope. The rope she holds refers to a cradle, but it is known that Van Gogh was influenced, when painting this portrait, by a book about the fishermen of Iceland, and he equated the wooden cradle rocked by the mother with the frail wooden vessel of the sailor rocked on the high seas. The symbolism that Van Gogh employed was also a strategy used with subtlety and confidence by Hamnett, in this work. The woman's uncompromising gaze, the rather oppressive decor of the room and sombre colour scheme, establish a powerful study of middle-class life.

Nina Hamnett

Major General
Bethune Lindsay
1919
—
Oil on canvas
127×91.94cm
National Gallery of
Canada Ottawa

Dolores
1931
—
Oil on canvas
91.44×50.8cm
Private Collection

P.89   Her portrait of the avant-garde sculptor Ossip Zadkine is a more straightforward presentation of a valued colleague. A note on the back dates it to June 1914 and Paris. Hamnett was intrigued by the contrast in her composition of the lively yet pensive head of the sculptor set in front of one of his recent works, a bold angular – and anguished – sculpted head in wood. The colour range she uses is one that would have been familiar to Zadkine as he worked in both wood and stone; browns, greys and a warm black, with the brightest note of red being accorded to Zadkine's generous mouth. Both 'heads' cast shadows on to the back wall of the room and this gives a halo effect to Zadkine's head. The large area of black of his roll-neck sweater (a surprisingly modern Bohemian image) is complemented by his pudding-basin hairstyle; Zadkine apparently cut Nina's hair in the same way. The corner of a set of bookshelves fills the bottom left-hand section of the painting; Hamnett was very fond of including strong forms around her sitters as if to reinforce their characters and also to set them in a context. They can be seen again in her portrait of

P.90   her painter friend, Dolores Courtney, whom she met at the Omega Workshops. These strong shapes were also something that Roger Fry employed in his portraits, but Hamnett was the more successful exponent of such a device. Charles Marriott, the highly influential critic of *The Times* during the 1910s and 1920s, wrote about Nina Hamnett's propensity for this method of building up a composition:

> Her planes and volumes do not look as if they were put in to make the design more difficult, but rather as if they were obvious means of making it clearer, lending colour to the assertion that women are more practical than men[12]

In 1921 she met an intriguing character at the Café Parnasse in

P.91   Paris, whom she painted Gentleman With a Top Hat. The sitter, George Manuel Unwin, introduced himself as a Chilean who had come to Paris to become an opera singer. He usually wore a top hat and spats, with a monocle and a cane, and his fashionable accessories are all included in her portrait of him. This was one of her largest portraits, and she portrayed George Unwin full-length (with his spats very prominent) and seated in a corner of her Paris studio. She has surrounded him with interesting shapes, some cut off by the edge of the canvas; a Moroccan rug hangs at upper left, the lower half of Nina Hamnett's guitar (an important studio prop and a crucial part of her social persona) shows at upper right and a large white spouted jug protrudes into the picture space at bottom right. The studio floor is tilted up at an angle, making use of artistic licence, and this helps to project Mr Unwin forward and impress his elegant presence upon the viewer. Unwin confessed to Nina that he was actually quite broke and made a living by accompanying tourists round Paris on Cook's tours. His smart suit was practically the only clothes he owned. The element of façade – of constructing an appearance and projecting a social persona – together with Unwin's rather distinctive looks, clearly appealed to Hamnett's interest in people's eccentricities.

When interviewed about her work in 1928, Nina Hamnett stressed the importance of her line drawings and her portraiture, and singled out as her best work to date her commissioned portrait of MAJOR GENERAL WILLIAM BETHUNE LINDSAY, painted in 1919 for the Canadian War Memorials Fund. She would have been gratified to receive the commission in 1919 from the Canadian Government since it meant that she got a good fee and that she was regarded as a major figure in British art at that time. Over a hundred British painters and sculptors produced over four hundred works for the Canadian War Memorials Fund, which was set up to provide a visual record of the First World War. Augustus John was asked by the Canadians to produce large canvases and it is likely that he was instrumental in Hamnett's involvement. Only four other British women painters besides Hamnett were commissioned by the Canadians (the others were Laura Knight, Anna Airy, Clare Atwood and Flora Lion), so it is a measure of her standing in London art circles that she secured this major governmental commission. In her portrait of Major General Lindsay, Hamnett placed a map of Europe in a confrontational way, behind the large peaked cap of the officer, almost as though the countries were thought forms emanating from his head. Undertaking this commission and seating herself for work purposes across the other side of the soldier's large desk must have encouraged memories of her father and his philistine attitude to her career.

Treasured books of press-cuttings

On Nina Hamnett's death three volumes of press-cuttings about her life and work were saved from her rented flat in Maida Vale. These reveal just how often she was mentioned in the London, provincial and foreign press throughout her working life, and the clippings cover both paintings and drawings on public view and her social appearances on the London scene. Even though her two autobiographies relate how money was always short, she nevertheless managed to scrape enough together to subscribe to a top London press-cutting agency from 1916 until the late 1940s. This fact reveals that Nina Hamnett paid great attention to the critical reception of her work. Good reviews, which constitute the majority of the press-cuttings, are often marked up with a pencil as if to underline the importance to Hamnett of encouraging remarks. This touching archive of her career, disclosed by these documents (which she must have chosen to rescue from the remnants of her belongings when fire destroyed her rented rooms in Howland Street in 1947) points up the paradox of her portrayal as an artist who appeared not to care about her work and wasted her talent.

The present whereabouts of much of the work recorded in these press-cutting albums is not known, but this is not unique to Hamnett. Many British artists' personal records which cover the years of the 1910s and 1920s, for example Roger Fry and Edward Wadsworth, also point up the same percentage of lost work. Hamnett's two autobiographies are thus doubly valuable, constituting a frank account of the life of a woman artist and assisting in the identification and recovery of her work.

1916, the year that the press cuttings begin, was the year when her professional career really took off and she started getting critical reviews, although she had been exhibiting her work in major mixed exhibitions, such as the New English Art Club and the Allied Artists' Association from the summer of 1913. In *Laughing Torso,* she recalled how the three portraits she sent to the Allied Artists' Association were hung in a group 'and I thought they looked very nice.... I had two press cuttings, one in *The Times,* of which I was very proud[13]'. She also took care to have her paintings professionally photographed by a photographer called Rendall who worked from Fitzroy Street, and these were stuck into the press-cutting volumes with details of their purchase, exhibition history and price of sale. Paintings that were destroyed were also noted in these volumes. A painting of a canal side urban view was accompanied by the annotation 'Destroyed Thank God' although it did not fall much below her normal standards. Her self-portrait, painted in 1913, and reproduced in the avant-garde London art magazine *Colour* in June 1915, was also destroyed according to the note beside its photograph in her press-cutting volumes.

A small section of one of the press-cutting volumes is devoted to a list of prices and buyers of her work. This list appears not to have been maintained for too long (it covers parts of 1919-20) but it does reveal that the more important members of the London art world at the time, such as Roger Fry, Sir Michael Sadler, the painters Jacob Kramer, Augustus John and Matthew Smith, and the art historian Tancred Borenius bought from Nina Hamnett. The management of money was perhaps something she put as a low priority, spending it freely and generously when she had it, living penuriously when she didn't. Basil Bunting drew attention to this aspect of her way of life: 'Nina Hamnett subsists miraculously by rare falls of manna on the stormy coast of Bohemia[14]'.

Sometime in the late 1940s or early 1950s Nina Hamnett went through her press-cutting albums, possibly when she was writing *Is She a Lady?,* and added wry and telling comments to some of the clippings.

These do show that she would have liked to have been more successful in her career, and that she suffered pangs of regret for lost opportunities. A comment by a reproduction of a powerful pencil sketch of an old lady's face dated 1908 stated: 'This was done by me at [the sketch class] at the London School of Art … when I was 18. It was a pity that I had no one to back me in those days otherwise I might have been Dame Laura Hamnett!'. A further comment dated 1953 and appended to a review of an exhibition she had had of recent watercolours of Paris cafés and streets, at the Independent Gallery in May 1921, was also rueful: 'Very good watercolours but before their time, sold only one! If I had had it now, they would probably be hailed as works of genius!'. In fact, as we have seen, Hamnett did benefit from the patronage and encouragement of figures such Sickert, Fry, and John, and her early career was promising and successful. Hamnett's own recklessness undoubtedly contributed to the decline of her career - she did not have the same dedication and professionalism as Laura Knight - but that is not the only reason. Hamnett had no one on a domestic level to support her - she lived alone, generally in a financially precarious state and often went hungry (a friend, Sheelah Hynes remembers how Nina had to avoid walking past baker's shops, the smell of fresh bread was too overwhelming). Although such conditions fulfill the popular mythology of artists starving in a garret, in reality they are not conducive to producing good work, or even having the means to do so. Added to this was the fact that by the middle to late 30's, Nina Hamnett was virtually an alcoholic, her life increasingly centred around the pubs and drinking clubs of Soho. Another reason was quite simply the fact that she was a woman and the difference this made to her status as an artist.

Lifestyle and reputation: Queen of Bohemia

When Nina Hamnett met Augustus John in the Café Royal around 1913, they were delighted to discover their mutual Welsh background, both having been born in Tenby and taught by the same school teachers. This produced a firm friendship which lasted the whole of Hamnett's life. In a way she was the female counterpart to Augustus John. He was regarded as an artist of prodigious talent, capable of both excellent draughtsmanship and paintings. Like Nina, he lived the life of a Bohemian to the full. The derivation of the word Bohemian comes from the word for a gipsy and so implied a wandering lifestyle with a living eked out from whatever natural talents could be utilised. It also suggested the avoidance of a cosy domestic home and so-called normal family life. Augustus John married twice, had many children and was notorious for his appetite for sex, drink and travel. Nina Hamnett danced naked at studio parties, took a series of lovers throughout her life, being especially fond of boxers and sailors, and also had an inextinguishable taste for alcohol and travel. The difference was that John, being a man, could lead the life of a rouée with social endorsement; his philandering seen as an acceptable attribute to his masculinity. 'Promiscuity' and hard drinking have more negative connotations for women. Furthermore John had the comfort and support of a home to return to. (Both his wives, Ida Nettleship and Dorelia – Dorothy McNeil – were artists who stopped painting once the demands of running a home and bringing up children took precedence.)

Nina Hamnett wrote two volumes of autobiographical reminiscences, *Laughing Torso* published in 1932 and *Is She a Lady?* published in 1955, using material from the diaries which she kept throughout her life. The frankness with which she wrote about her unconventional lifestyle led to enormous publicity, the press both scandalized and fascinated by her racy style and straightforward account of Bohemian life. Her fame was consolidated by a court case when the magician Aleister Crowley (a former friend) sued Hamnett and her publishers, Constable, for libel. The case attracted a lot of media attention with its allegations of black magic and satanism. Crowley lost the case, but it added to his – and by association – Nina's notoriety.

In the press coverage which followed the publication of Nina Hamnett's second volume of autobiography, *Is She a Lady?*, she began to gain the title of 'Queen of Bohemia'. Indeed, the recent biography of her life and work by Denise Hooker, published in 1986, uses this phrase as its subtitle. On the inside of the dust-wrapper of the second volume of Michael Holroyd's biography of Augustus John, published in 1975, Holroyd uses the phrase 'King of British Bohemia' for John, although it does not appear again beyond this dust-wrapper. John did not need the phrase to help in the identification or codification of his life and work, whereas there is the danger of it becoming a superficial handle with which to classify Nina Hamnett. 'We are the sort of people our fathers warned us against', John is reputed to have said to Nina Hamnett, thus recognizing that she was leading the same lifestyle as himself. Hamnett appears to be poking fun at her situation by daring to entitle her second volume of autobiographical writings *Is She a Lady?* since it begs an answer to the rhetorically posed question, which is either yes or no. From the evidence of the lifestyle described within the book, most of the British public would have answered 'no'. Hamnett wrote in *Laughing Torso*, 'a lady was the last thing that I wanted to be[15].'

The years of life and work covered by *Is She a Lady?* were those from circa 1925, when *Laughing Torso* ended, to the late 1940s. Hamnett's least productive period was from about 1932, when *Laughing Torso* was published, until 1943, thus comprising the central years of *Is She a Lady?*.

The ten years from 1932 were those in which she came closest to leading the life of a gipsy and her artistic output dwindled dramatically. She does not appear to have exhibited anything between summer 1936 and August 1943, and since her exhibition record is closely allied to her work output, she may well have not produced anything in those years which she thought was equal to the standard she had earlier set for herself. It is not difficult to imagine how this situation came about. The practice of art is not unlike the profession of a ballet dancer or a musician; regular application is necessary for the professional talents to remain at the fingertips. If the practice is abandoned for a short while, perhaps through illness or a change in personal domestic circumstances, then it becomes harder to resume. Hamnett did not function as a professional artist for a period of about ten years. The flamboyant social side of her personality came to the fore and eclipsed the serious and dedicated painter. It may have even become a kind of vicious circle; the more she enjoyed herself the more she felt guilty at neglecting her talents, and she determined to enjoy herself even more to expunge any sense of culpability or failure in terms of her career. One senses, however, a sort of desperation to her life at this time, accounts of her routine[16] stress her straightened circumstances, increasing reliance on drink, and perhaps too an understandable tendency to live in the past, her many stories of friendships with famous personalities becoming a sort of 'party piece', regaled for the price of a gin. Nevertheless Hamnett clearly became a symbolic figure for a new generation of artists and writers who met her in the pubs of Soho in the 1950s (like Francis Bacon, Lucian Freud, Robert Colquhoun, John Minton, John Heath-Stubbs) who respected her links to a past 'real' Bohemia. To the end Nina Hamnett retained her toughness and ascerbity, always ready with a pithy witticism and gallantly maintaining her role as social patron, albeit a patron without means.

But Hamnett in fact never *entirely* stopped working and had a kind of second wind in the late 1940s and early 1950s. Many drawings from this period testify to her still strong skills as a draughtsman. As always, her best work came out of observation of her immediate social environment and she produced some poignant drawings of old ladies in London pubs studying the *Daily Mirror,* half a pint of stout to hand.

Augustus John also suffered a decline in his talent. But his longevity and public profile ensured veneration; he became a Royal Academician, finally gaining the highest establishment award of the Order of Merit. Nina Hamnett died in hospital at the age of sixty-six after falling from the window of her flat. She was in poor health after breaking her thigh in 1953. She died alone and in extreme poverty. When John died he was acknowledged as a national figure and his death marked the passing of an era. Nina Hamnett, on the other hand, just quietly disappeared from view as an artistic personality, although her social activities were recorded in passing in most of the biographies and documentaries of life in Britain during the period between the two World Wars.

Since her death in 1956, or more accurately since the publication of her two autobiographies, her fame as a social character has overshadowed her artistic career. Her obituary in *The Times* pondered:

> It is an open question whether the world gained or lost by the partial sacrifice of Nina Hamnett, the painter of portraits and landscapes, and illustrator, to Nina Hamnett, the Bohemian, but readers of her book of reminiscences, *Laughing Torso*, will have no doubt that in the latter role she contributed to the gaiety of nations. Her friends will know something more: that whatever she might have done ultimately in painting if she had stuck to it more closely, Miss Hamnett was a complete success as a person; generous, good-humoured, loyal and witty.

Nina Hamnett lived her life in a way associated with a 'masculine' form of independence; she had very few family ties, she was not dependent on anybody and nobody was dependent on her, she had no interest in home-making, cooking, and other domestic skills. She liked the social and communal aspects of pub life, she had a wide range of acquaintances rather than a few close friends, and she was quite capable of launching herself into strange company and making herself accepted. People responded to Nina because she was dashing and outrageous; she broke taboos of femininity and conventional morality and refused to be constrained by the limitations expected of a woman. But in placing her life and work before the public gaze she made herself vulnerable. Now that we can see Hamnett's career as an artist in a clearer light, to 'a complete success as a person' should be added, 'considerable success as a painter'. Although she is a hard act to follow, her example is invigorating.

Nina Hamnett

DORA CARRINGTON
WITH HER CAT
HAM SPRAY
c.1927
—
TATE GALLERY
ARCHIVE

CARRINGTON
1893 - 1932

'It's rather maddening to have the ambition of
Tintoretto and to paint like a diseased
dormouse.'

Of the five painters in this book, Carrington's life and career underlines
most sharply the contradictions involved in being a female artist. Until
recently she was not recognized as an artist at all: her fame, such as it was,
came from her involvement with the Bloomsbury 'group'.

Much of the fascination with the history of the Bloomsbury circle
lies in its appeal as an upper-middle class soap opera. The plot of this real
life drama centred on a small and exclusive group of intellectuals, writers,
artists and academics. Their friendships, love affairs, feuds, philosophies
and beliefs, have formed the basis of a wave of books published by and
about Bloomsbury personalities in the last twenty years.[1]

Carrington featured quite heavily in this Bloomsbury revival
because certain facts about her life made her an interesting dramatic
protagonist. Firstly she lived with, and devoted herself to the writer and
biographer Lytton Strachey, who was seventeen years older than her and
homosexual. Secondly when he died of cancer she killed herself at the age
of 39. And lastly her love for Lytton did not stop her having a number of
other, rather complicated relationships with both men and women.

This led to Carrington acquiring a somewhat misleading
reputation as a 'femme fatale', and it is in this role, rather than as a
painter, that she has been most widely known and judged, the cult of the
Bloomsbury personality suppressing an understanding of Carrington as
an artist. In recent years, however, there has been a steadily growing
interest in her work and a realization that she was more than a
Bloomsbury *ingénue*.

When Carrington's own letters were published[2], they shed light on
her complex and compelling personality and left many readers intrigued
and impressed by the directness of her writing, her humour and vitality.
But there was also a more negative side to her character; Carrington was
her own best analyst and her letters and diaries reveal the doubt and
insecurity which beset her. She constantly belittles her own achievements
and projects the image of a failed artist. In fact, her painting and
decorative work displays a sensitive assurance and witty originality which
makes her an artist to be taken seriously.

Ironically, for someone who has consistently provoked a
considerable amount of public interest (there are plans to make a feature
film about her life), Carrington was an intensely private person and

this is another reason why her work has been little seen; she was exceedingly reluctant to exhibit it. Discovering her work therefore is like uncovering a lovely piece of wallpaper under layers of old paint; there is a sense of excitement generated by finding such richness in an unexpected place combined with a desire to find out more about the history of this mysterious discovery.

Who was Dora Carrington?

Carrington, by all accounts, was an exceptionally difficult person to know – ambiguous, secretive and elusive are some of the adjectives frequently applied to her. Paradoxically, she also appeared in her letters and conversations with friends to be demonstrative, witty and easily able to establish a close rapport with those she liked. Her diffidence and evasiveness is evident in photographs – her head often tilted down or away from the camera, face half hidden behind her hair – although there are also pictures – mostly of a younger Carrington – which show her exuberant and in high spirits. There is a 'little girl' aspect to her appearance, even in her late thirties Carrington wore print dresses and white ankle socks, expressive of an ambiguity she felt about her sexuality.

Many people who knew her testify to Carrington's charm, her very individual and idiosyncratic style, and her teasing and flattering interest in her friends, 'I still think of her as the closest friend I had, but I think she made everybody that she cared for feel that they were tremendously important to her'[3]. Her work too has a very personal aspect; some of Carrington's best paintings are portraits of people she knew well and much of her decorative work was undertaken for her friends. But it isn't just that her main creative energies found expression within a domestic context; Carrington's aesthetic was both theatrical and intimate – she loved *transforming* objects and people. Many of her decorations contain jokes and puns, and her paintings of people and places have a psychological intensity which reveals the passion she felt about them and an understanding – or 'reading' – of their character.

Carrington's father Samuel Carrington spent long periods in India, building railways for the East Indian Company, and he didn't marry until he retired in his fifties. His wife was Charlotte Houghton who had been a governess. The family moved a lot, but eventually settled in Bedford and Dora was the fourth of five children. As an adult she always wrote very fondly of her father, but was deeply critical of her mother, whose pursuit of bourgeois respectability she despised. Carrington felt that her mother had insensitively thwarted her father's individuality. After his death, in 1918, she wrote to Lytton, 'I know my mother cared and is unhappy. But I can't forgive her for taming him as she did, and for regarding all his

Lytton Strachey
with Carrington
Ham Spray
c.1926
—

Portrait of
Catharine
Carrington
1926
—

Oil on canvas
40.64×30.48cm
Private collection

independence and wildness as "peculiarities" and just making out he was a sentimental good husband.'

Carrington had, herself, a strong desire for independence, and studying at the Slade School of Art in London brought with it the freedom to live away from home. She attended the Slade from 1910 to 1914 and was one of the first students to crop her hair, moving away from a nineteenth-century image of womanhood – long hair worn 'up' in a bun – to a more modern, clean-cut look (Nina Hamnett went through a similar process of transformation). She also dropped her hated first name, Dora, and insisted on being called just Carrington. Many of the women students at the Slade took on this 'masculine' identification in order to be considered as serious in their work as their male colleagues. But the fact that Carrington retained this name throughout her life is an indication of the ambivalence she felt about femininity and an expression of her desire to continue living and working independently. When, in 1921, she reluctantly consented to marry Ralph Partridge, she wrote to Gerald Brenan, 'To you I shall ever be Carrington *and* to myself'.

Reputations

When Carrington was at the Slade the teaching of art was dominated by the formidable Professor Tonks, whose exacting standards of draughtsmanship imposed a highly linear technique. Although it has since been discredited, this approach formed an important basis for many painters, Stanley Spencer and Paul Nash for instance, who though they may have gone on to work in a far more experimental manner, often used an iconographic depiction. This is evident in Carrington's own work; her painting and drawing has a consistent foundation of fine detail. Because Carrington's work has been little exhibited, her place in a British tradition of early twentieth-century painting has not been recognised.

There is a photograph dating from Carrington's period at the Slade which shows her sitting with her contemporaries, a group which included Stanley Spencer, Mark Gertler, David Bomberg and Christopher Nevinson. Although none of these painters had easy, unproblematic careers – Gertler and Bomberg in particular suffered from critical antagonism which contained elements of anti-semitism – they have recently been recognized as among the most important and innovative British painters of the early twentieth century[4]. Carrington, on the other hand is regarded, at best, as a minor talent. Yet when Carrington was at the Slade she was considered a very skilled student and was awarded a Slade Scholarship as well as winning four prizes over the four years she attended the school. Although Carrington's own diffidence hampered her from attaining professional recognition as an artist later in her career, what happened after art school – or more precisely what didn't happen – encapsulates the experiences of many promising women students. At art school they frequently equalled or outshone their male contemporaries, but in the external context of dealers, exhibitions and patrons, a conventional chauvinism dominated and male artists were privileged over women. Such a pattern meant that it was that much more difficult to establish oneself *as* an artist and women were more likely to have to work in isolation.

During her time at the Slade and the immediate pre-war period, Carrington had friends among other women students at the Slade such as Dorothy Brett, Barbara Hiles, Constance Lane; and both John Nash and Mark Gertler were enthusiastic suitors. With Nash, she maintained an affectionate friendship and appears to have successfully diverted his romantic interest in her, by introducing him to Christine Kuhlenthal, a fellow student at the Slade who later married him. Nash is usually cited as an important influence on Carrington, and aspects of her landscape paintings have similarities to his. However, it was not necessarily a one-way process. *Her* influence on his development as a painter was arguably just as significant. A watercolour of Carrington's called HILLS IN THE SNOW AT HURSTBOURNE TARRANT (1916) anticipates the direction Nash's work was to take a few years later. At one time sold as a John Nash picture, it was Nash himself who recognized it as a Carrington. Hurstbourne Tarrant was where Carrington's parents moved to from Bedford and she evidently painted it when staying there.

The picture has a semi-circular design rather like the effect of a fish-eye lens, with the sky almost missed out and the top of the hill forming a rounded horizon. Like all Carrington's best landscape studies, it has a surreal intensity. The statuesque bare trees, with their shadows falling across the snow, have an expressive, almost human character. In an equally expressive phrase, she described the same view in a letter to Mark Gertler 'the ridge of the hill opposite stands up hard and sharp like the backbone of a whale'. Landscape becomes more than a decorative representation of the English countryside, and shapes, indentations, texture and patterns take on a more forceful composition. Carrington is part of a tradition of visionary landscape artists, like Samuel Palmer and William Blake in the nineteenth century, and in the twentieth century John Nash and his brother Paul, and Stanley Spencer, who relate landscape and place to unconscious dreams and images.

P.96,130 This element of Carrington's work is most strongly evident in THE MILL AT TIDMARSH, BERKSHIRE (1918), and MOUNTAIN RANGES FROM YEGEN, ANDALUSIA (1924). Both use strong deep colours and a patina of detail which builds the paintings into an expressive, and *psychological* response to a particular place. Both were locations personally significant to Carrington; Tidmarsh Mill was where she lived with Strachey for six years, and Yegen was where Gerald Brenan lived in Spain and which Carrington visited several times. THE MILL has vivid orange roofs which are reflected in a mirror-like mill pond, and this warm light combined with the blue patches of sky, create a heightened, glowing painting. The Spanish painting is even more extraordinary, the hills are oddly reminiscent of knees under a bedspread, while the distant mountains have the texture of a prehistoric monster. The juxtaposition of these strange, unsettling images, work to produce a surreal landscape which at the same time is very friendly. Carrington wrote to Brenan, when she was painting it, about experimenting with a new technique, 'I am trying a new plan, an entire under-painting in brilliant colours, over which I shall glaze green and more transparent colours'. This building up of layers of paint was very successful in the representation of light and shade, and the way sunlight hits the sculptural forms of the hills.

Carrington's relationship with Mark Gertler which started when they were at the Slade and continued in an intermittent way for some years, was a protracted affair, with a number of rather torturous twists and turns. Gertler was from a Jewish family who settled in Whitechapel after emigrating to Britain from Middle Europe. With the help of William Rothenstein, he obtained funding from the Jewish Educational Aid Society, and was able to attend the Slade. Their relationship was marked by sexual tension – he made demands she was reluctant to fulfil – and conflict over the role two artists of the opposite sex were expected to perform. Gertler could be encouraging to Carrington about her work but he was not above the odd provocative jibe: 'You certainly should learn something about cooking. I should always expect my girlfriends to be better cooks than artists. Don't let this annoy you....'[5] Carrington was obviously not prepared to undertake the nurturing role Gertler expected of her, although she did manage to sustain their relationship as an uneasy friendship long after she went to live with Lytton Strachey (Gertler expressed his disgust at this move with vehemence).

This inequality of expectation was mirrored in external circumstances. Carrington showed Roger Fry some of her work around this time, and was discouraged by his response. Gertler on the other hand was 'taken up' and encouraged by art critics such as Fry and Rothenstein, when he left the Slade.

Making Murals

After leaving art school in 1914 Carrington did some private teaching in order to earn her own income, and undertook decorative commissions.

Her interest in decorative work had started earlier; when she was

ZADKINE (PORTRAIT OF
OSSIP ZADKINE)
1914
—
OIL ON CANVAS
78.74×78.74cm
PRIVATE COLLECTION

STILL LIFE NO 1
c.1915
—
OIL ON CANVAS
34.92×25.4cm
COURTESY OF EDWARD
BOOTH-CLIBBORN

Nina Hamnett

THE STUDENT
(DOLORES COURTNEY)
1917
—
OIL ON CANVAS
81.28×60.96cm
FERENS ART GALLERY:
HULL CITY MUSEUMS
& ART GALLERY

DER STURM
c.1915
—
OIL ON CANVAS
54.61×40cm
COURTESY OF EDWARD
BOOTH-CLIBBORN

GENTLEMAN WITH A
TOP HAT
c.1921
—
OIL ON CANVAS
144.78×95.88cm
COURTESY OF EDWARD
BOOTH-CLIBBORN

THE RING MASTER
c.1918
—
OIL ON CANVAS
73.02×50.8cm
COURTESY OF EDWARD
BOOTH-CLIBBORN

Nina Hamnett

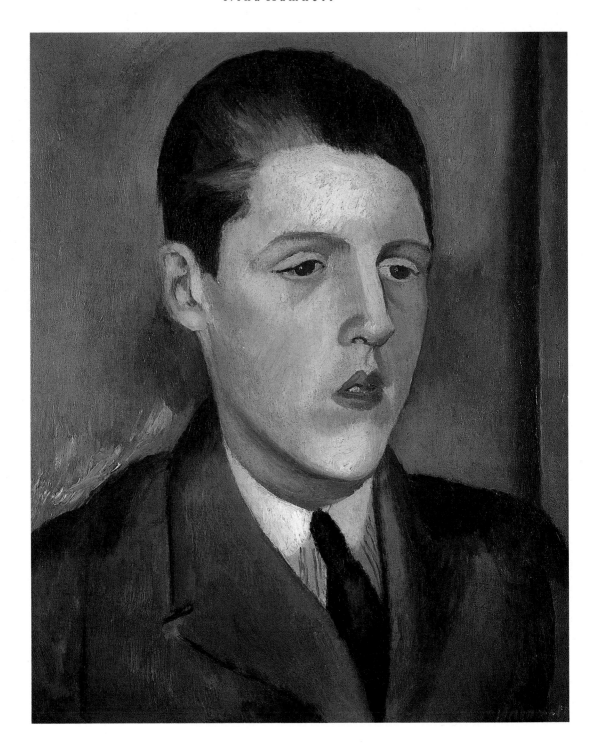

RUPERT DOONE
1922-23
—
OIL ON CANVAS
40.64×27.94cm
DONCASTER MUSEUM
& ART GALLERY

JAMES HEPBURN
1922
—
OIL ON CANVAS
40.64×27.94cm
PRIVATE COLLECTION

Nina Hamnett

A BENCH
IN REGENT'S PARK
1930
—
WATERCOLOUR
29.21×21.59cm
PRIVATE COLLECTION

GILES LYTTON
STRACHEY
1916
—
OIL ON CANVAS
71.1×101.6cm
PRIVATE COLLECTION

ANNIE
c.1917
—
OIL ON CANVAS
50.8×40.6cm
PRIVATE COLLECTION

MOUNTAIN RANGES
FROM YEGEN,
ANDALUSIA
1924
—
OIL ON CANVAS
68.6×78.7cm
PRIVATE COLLECTION

PAINTED GRAMOPHONE
c.1928
—
93×48.3×50.2cm
PAINTED FOR ALIX
STRACHEY
PORTSMOUTH CITY
MUSEUM & ART
GALLERY

HILLS IN SNOW AT
HURSTBOURNE
TARRANT
1916

—

WATERCOLOUR
53.97×64.13cm
PRIVATE COLLECTION

—

MARK GERTLER IN
FANCY-DRESS

—

at the Slade she and John Nash attended an evening class in the art of fresco painting[6], which included practical instruction on how to prepare walls and plaster them. In 1912 she painted three fresco panels with Constance Lane, at Ashridge House in Hertfordshire (the job appears to have been a private commission, the panels are situated in a side building known as the Old School House). They are all of rural scenes, PICKING VEGETABLES, SHEEP SHEARING, and HAY MAKING. Carrington wrote to John Nash that she was 'drawing the big cartoon hard. 6ft by 5ft. It *is* a job. But so exciting. I spend the mornings in the fields drawing big heavy elms for it and small village boys come and pose in the garden in the evening.' PICKING VEGETABLES, the panel that Carrington was working on, shows two men hoeing vegetables, with a woman and two children looking on. Carrington's detailed depiction of the vegetables, the dramatic use of landscape in the rolling hills in the background and the 'big heavy' elm trees, are characteristic of her style, although the proportion of the child and rather static pose of the woman, are not as assured as her later figurative work. The colour scheme is predominantly muted greens and blues, with yellow and oranges providing contrasting detail. Carrington went back to visit the frescoes in 1925 and was pleased to find them unchanged, commenting to Gerald Brenan in a letter, 'They are still intact, and haven't fallen down or changed colour which just proves that frescoes can last in England, which everyone always denies'. They are fortunately still intact today; one of the panels suffered some damage from damp, but Ashridge House, now a Management College, has had them restored.

There were plans to do further fresco work. With John and Paul Nash, Carrington was going to decorate the walls of a church in Uxbridge, but objections from church elders combined with the start of the First World War, meant the project was shelved. Carrington was also involved in plans to decorate a village hall in Dorset for Sir Ernest Debenham's 'model' village, Bladen Valley, but again this did not come to fruition.

Decorative work became an important creative outlet for Carrington and like Vanessa Bell and Duncan Grant's decorative schemes at Charleston Farmhouse, much of her work was inspired by and centred on a domestic setting. Simply to list the amount of decorative work that Carrington accomplished gives an indication of the importance it has in evaluating her career: woodcuts, pub signs, painted tiles, glass pictures, *trompe l'œil* panels, book illustrations; painted china and lampshades, tiled fireplaces, decorative door panels; painted trunks, trays, chests, ashtrays, a gramophone, a bed. Not all of these have survived[7]; many would have been in daily use and were not designed anyway as 'works of art', but as playful adaptations of everyday items. Fortunately, enough of her work *is* still in existence for us to see how original, idiosyncratic, and inventive she was. Carrington's decorative work has a relationship to the work being undertaken at the Omega Workshops at a similar period; she was working independently in the same direction and clearly saw similar possibilities in the decorative arts.

Painted Surfaces

The Omega Workshops were started in 1913 by Roger Fry who had been instrumental in bringing the work of the European Post-Impressionists to Britain. He organized an exhibition of their work in 1910 at the Grafton Galleries, London, and a second exhibition two years later. The impact of these shows was significant; the work of Derain, Manet, Matisse, Van Gogh, Gauguin, and Picasso had been little seen outside France and caused a scandal, most British critics responding with shock to the wild colours and abstract formal concerns of much of the work.

For artists interested in embracing this radical approach, the impact of Post-Impressionism was liberating, and initiated a much more experimental attitude to subject, form, and colour. Roger Fry helped to keep this momentum going by writing about the importance of *form* over subject matter[8], and constructing this into an aesthetic theory which had a profound, though not always positive, effect on the way British art has been valued and understood[9]. And Fry's enthusiasm and practical bent, ensured that there was suddenly a new sense of direction, and just as importantly, a feeling of excitement, about what was possible in modern painting.

Work by British artists was included in the Second Post-Impressionist Exhibition, and the following year the Omega Workshops were set up. The idea was to provide a source of income for artists willing to undertake decorative commissions, and to shake up the foundations of good taste in interior design. As well as interior decoration, much of which used mural design, the workshops designed furniture, and decorated household objects – bowls, jugs, plates, trays, boxes, vases, lampshades, screens – as well as textiles, curtains, cushion covers and soft furnishings.

The Omega Workshop did not prove to be profitable as a business venture and folded after six years, but the ideas behind it, and the sheer freedom with which visual images could be given a practical application, has had a long-standing influence[10]. Carrington has not been credited with having any involvement with Omega although given her friendship with many of the people involved with the workshops, plus her own interest in decorative work, it is highly likely that she contributed some designs. In 1917 she produced four woodcut illustrations for the very first

PANDORA'S BOX
c.1920

———

SET OF FIREPLACE
TILES
1930

———

PAINTED FOR ALEC AND
FRANCES PENROSE,
ORIGINALLY FOR THEIR
HOUSE IN LONDON
100×96cm
PRIVATE COLLECTION

DECORATIONS FOR
DR GEORGE RYLANDS'
ROOMS IN KING'S
COLLEGE CAMBRIDGE
1928

———

book produced by the Hogarth Press; *Two Stories* was written by Virginia Woolf and her husband Leonard, the founders of Hogarth.

Carrington's work was developing anyway along similar aesthetic lines to Omega, and, as we shall see, her particular contribution to decorative design fused the modern concepts associated with Omega with an interest in older traditions of English folk-art.

Home-work

> There are so many things for me to do. A lampshade to design, a dresser to paint yellow; Lytton's bed to paint. Two woodcuts to make, and at least forty letters to write before Christmas. [11]

Carrington lived with Lytton Strachey from the end of 1917, until his death in 1931. When she met him in 1915 he was writing *Eminent Victorians*, the book which was to make his name as a biographer and critic. At the time however, he was struggling with ill-health and lack of money, and a group of his friends banded together to try and establish some sort of support and security on his behalf. Carrington became involved in this scheme and set out to find him a place to live in the country, but within reach of London. Whether she originally planned to live with him there is unclear, but that is how it turned out.

After much searching, she found Tidmarsh Mill near Reading, in Berkshire. They lived here until 1924, when they moved to Ham Spray House in Wiltshire. This started a pattern of 'looking after Lytton' which for Carrington became a lifetime's work; these two houses were homes on which she expended a great deal of emotional and creative energy. In a sense they became her main creative outlet.

In some ways Carrington's move to the country signified a retreat from competing in the contemporary art scene, but at the same time she was able to create a larger 'canvas' for herself to paint and decorate; as well as her own homes there were those of her friends. She was constantly undertaking commissions and many of her letters complain at all the work she is faced with. To Margaret Waley she wrote, 'My gluttony for earning a little money has paid me out. I am sick of Tiles. All last week in that lovely heat, drew Bird after Bird, flower after flower, and now this week there are three more fireplaces to do. The Franklin's will never guess what Bloody Sweat went to produce these trifles light as air.[12]'

Carrington's idiosyncratic touch is evident in the household objects which she transformed into decorative extravaganzas. For example there is something she called 'Pandora's Box', the bottom half of a grandfather clock which she made into a cupboard, decorating the glass sides and front with coloured inks and silver paper. Diana Mosley describes a 'rococo fantasy of shells she gave us; it was mounted on a painted wooden base which she said once belonged to a sewing machine'[13]. It was also for Diana Mosley that she painted a *trompe l'œil* window as a surprise and to celebrate Diana's return home after the birth of her son. It shows a cook, dressed in mob cap and eighteenth-century-style clothes, sitting behind the 'fake' window, demurely peeling an apple; on the table sits a cat who is staring up at a canary in a cage. The domestic details and period setting is appropriate for the Queen Anne House where the window is situated.

This work illustrates a difference between Carrington's approach to decorative art, and that taken by Duncan Grant and Vanessa Bell at Charleston. Their joint work was very consciously an extension of the Omega tradition and Post-Impressionist style; furniture, walls, doors, curtains, cushions, and so on, were covered in their distinctive flowing lines and rich colours. Carrington tended to look back to older decorative traditions; sometimes adopting a self-conscious pastiche of conventions and conceits, an expression of the wit and humour which was intrinsic to her style. There is for example, still in existence at Ham Spray, a *trompe l'œil* bookcase – actually a door – where each 'book' is bound in hand-blocked paper that she made herself. The titles are puns on real books and authors and refer to the illusionistic 'deceit' of the *trompe l'œil;* 'False Appearances by Dora Wood', 'Deception by Jane Austen', 'On The Shelf Vols I & II', 'The Empty Room by Virginia Woolf', 'The Hollow Wood by Iris Tree', and so on. The painstaking detail that she took to carry out these elaborate jokes and decorative schemes, are characteristic of her approach to life, which made her, as many of her friends have testified, such an amusing and sympathetic companion. She decorated two sets of built-in drawers for Dorelia John, with identifying labels, 'Tools & Nails', 'Twine & String', 'Silks & Cotton', 'Writing Paper' and so on, but also, more mischievously, 'Cats & Kittens', and 'Rags & Bones'.

Another difference between the Charleston aesthetic and Carrington's approach, was the care she took in researching and discovering methods of design. She was constantly experimenting with different techniques, 'Oh but I made a new discovery yesterday – a way of printing patterns on leather with dyes,' she writes to Lytton. Carrington's style was more circumspect than Bell's and Grant's at Charleston – there every surface becomes a possible place for a visual image – whereas Carrington's work was generally tailored to a traditional decorative scheme, within which she would make witty innovations. She made a tiled fireplace for Alec and Frances Penrose for their wedding, which is in a Dutch delft-style, but incorporates elements of their family history and a visual pun on their names; a rose crossed with a fountain pen is heralded by the motto 'No Rose Without A Pen'.

P.132

Carrington's reputation as a rather tragic figure has eclipsed one of the most attractive aspects of her personality – and which finds expression in her work – her sense of humour. This is particularly evident in her correspondence, not only in her descriptions of people and situations, but most exuberantly, in her sketches which crop up throughout the letters. Many of these act as a parody of her relationship with Lytton; he and she are transposed into various different guises. Numerous illustrations from her letters also place Carrington as a rival to Gwen John in the iconography of cats; again these are cats transformed into amusing companions, humanized creatures who re-enact Carrington's domestic duties.

Carrington's images tend to be pictorial in a narrative tradition; 'I started a decoration of the cellar door yesterday. It looks exquisite. A vineyard scene with Boozing Youths and a fox contemplating the grapes', she writes in a letter to Lytton in 1925. Hunting scenes, nymphs, fishes, shells, flowers, ships, archers, birds, vases, urns, ribbons and bows, are some of her recurring motifs. Swagged curtains in particular appear again and again in her pictures, testifying to the idea of facade and theatricality that so fascinated her. It is as if – as with her use of *trompe l'œil* – Carrington is foregrounding the illusionistic nature of picture making and playing on its conventions.

In 1928 Carrington undertook the decoration of Dr George Rylands' rooms in King's College, Cambridge. She painted four doors and a fireplace, partly basing her colour scheme on the apricots and grey-pinks of Ryland's collection of old china. Carrington made cut-out stencils for the main figures, which are classical torsos emerging from a cartouche – a scroll-like ornamental base – similar to the base of a statue, which is emblazoned with Rylands' initials. Around the door-frames, and acting as a visual frame for the figures, she painted an apricot base and drew the butt-end of her paintbrush through the wet paint to make squiggle designs. Both doors and fireplace incorporate cross-hatched smudged effects which maintain a delicate and lighthearted patterning. Seen today the decorations look surprisingly modern, echoing the contemporary fascination with decorative surfaces and pastiche copies of classical design.

One of her most successful, and unique decorative experiments was with glass pictures. She appears to have started making these in the mid-1920s, probably after having discovered some old Victorian glass paintings, or 'treacle prints' as they were sometimes called. Carrington collected all kinds of tinsel paper and silver foil. Sweet papers and the foil from cigarette packets were particularly prized because they had different textures. These were smoothed out onto a flat surface. She would then paint on them using coloured inks. This was then covered in glass, and

P.132

sometimes areas of the glass itself was shaded in with a matt paint. Because of the shiny and textured surface of the base of silver foil, as well as the translucent effect of the inks, the pictures reflect light, and shine when the light hits them from different directions. They were also a modest commercial success. She wrote to Alix Stachey[14]:

> You will be delighted to hear my ambitious nature is at last asserting itself. I now make over £3 a week selling little glass pictures at the Gerrard Street Book shop. The pictures only take 2 hours to make and some sell for 35/- or £2. So really the profit is enormous. My plan is to keep this minor talent as a means of making money in the winter, and in the spring and summer, do my serious painting. Flower pieces, Boxers, Balloons, volcanoes, tight rope dancers, Victorian Beauties, Soldiers, Tropical Botanical flowers, Birds and Fruits, are a few of my subjects.

Carrington took Victorian folk-art and combined it with the idea of genre painting to produce a very individual form of decorative art. She was also able to transpose the medium onto other surfaces, producing a pair of door panels decorated with painted silver paper in a tulip design, and her letters contain references to glass ashtrays made in the same way.

Carrington's diverse and inventive creativity led her to work in the decorative arts as well as in painting. But this has had adverse consequences for her reputation. Firstly her work cannot be easily labelled and categorized into traditional artistic pigeonholes. Secondly, the kind of decorative work she undertook was rarely taken very seriously or considered worthy of critical attention by art historians. Since most of Carrington's decorative work consisted of private commissions, they were not viewed and judged in the same way as public commissions. Much of her artistic output skirts the delicate boundary between, on the one hand, 'women's work', an extension of home decoration, or arts and crafts – and on the other, 'professional' artistic endeavour – that which can be exhibited in a gallery; in both cases she evaded critical attention.

Real Work

Carrington was always berating herself for not working hard enough at her 'serious' work, painting. 'If only I could paint what I want to, I should be completely happy.... But a blockage like a cold in the nose, seems to get between me and my brush' (letter to Lytton). Like most painters, she was continually dissatisfied with the work she produced, but her self-criticism took a rather extreme, though often comic, form: 'It's rather maddening to feel one ought to paint so much better than one does and to be filled with ideas and to, in reality produce messes that ought to

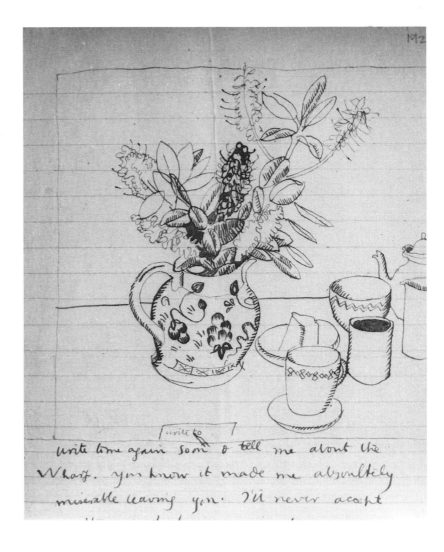

CACTUS
UNDATED
——
OIL ON CANVAS
45.72×76.72cm
PRIVATE COLLECTION

be consigned down the … (this sentence is completed by a picture of a lavatory)' (letter to Alix Strachey). Shortly before her suicide, Carrington wrote despairingly in her diary, 'Now I survey my life what do I see. My studio is a mirror of my existence on earth. Untidy, disorganized and incomplete.'

Carrington's painting had three main themes: portraits, landscapes, and flower compositions. As we have seen, her best landscape studies communicated an intense evocation of a place. Her flower paintings are perhaps her least exciting genre; they tend to be formally composed vases of flowers, Carrington's interest being the texture of leaves, petals and background, which she executed in a kind of pointillist technique, sometimes producing an image of startling simplicity such as Cactus. Some of her flower paintings reappear as motifs in the glass pictures, and similarly a glass picture design is used as a decoration on a dresser Carrington painted at Ham Spray.

It is as a portraitist that Carrington achieved unqualified success. Her portraits have a very solid physical presence, but are painted with sensitivity. Julia Strachey, Annie, Mrs Box, Boy With Concertina, Catherine Carrington, and the famous portrait of Giles Lytton Strachey, all show what a 'painterly' approach Carrington took. She used very fine brushstrokes, again in rather a pointillist style, to build up the form of the work, and in this way was able to achieve a highly subtle kind of colouring. Her portraits show a skilled combination of substance and delicacy; her sitters are very definitely and solidly placed before us, but what is being conveyed about the person and their character is intimate and percipient. Carrington side-steps the formality of most traditional portrait painting of her day and manages to 'get the point' of the person across in a direct way.

In the portraits Carrington tailors her colour schemes to suit the character of the sitter; her painting of her great friend Julia Strachey is carried out in delicate pastel shades of lilac, pale blue and green, and creamy pinks, and she has dressed her in turban and glittering necklace – a kind of twentieth-century princess – Carrington sometimes addressed her letters to 'Princess Julia' and liked to characterize her as an exotic oriental beauty. In her two portraits of Annie, who worked as cook and household help for Carrington, soft shades of blue and green predominate. Carrington places Annie right at the forefront of both pictures so that the solidity of her presence is very real, and yet the colouring and lighting of the pictures conveys her shyness. Her large picture of Mrs Box, a farmer whom Carrington painted on a holiday in Bude, Cornwall has a similar coherence though here the three-quarter length pose, traditional clothes and bonnet, and determined expression emphasize Mrs Box's tenacious strength, illuminated by a glowing orange

P.95

P.95

Carrington

BOY WITH CONCERTINA

1924

—

OIL ON CANVAS

63.5×50.8cm

PRIVATE COLLECTION

MRS BOX

1919

—

OIL ON CANVAS

91.4×76.2cm

PRIVATE COLLECTION

and brown palette.

Carrington painted several portraits of Lytton Strachey and in all of them he is reading a book. But undoubtedly her finest study of him is GILES LYTTON STRACHEY which is a close-up profile view with his extremely long hands holding a book, dominating the picture. The painting is sensitively executed and a fine study of Strachey's face, but it is the hands which add a unique touch and express the odd, eccentric appeal of this man who meant so much to Carrington. The way she has 'lit' the painting so that the pearly green background sets off the dark reds and browns of the figure, creates a very rich and intimate scene.

P.95

Painting, for Carrington, was a very private affair, and it was with extreme reluctance that she would send work to exhibitions. In the letters there are only a couple of references to submitting paintings to public shows, once to the London Group, and to the Grosvenor Galleries in 1921. Her diffidence seems to have been part lack of confidence and part hyper-sensitivity to criticism. She feared the frigidity of an objective analysis of something as personal as portrait painting. After completing Lytton's portrait, she wrote in her diary, 'Tonight it looks wonderfully good and I am happy. But I dread showing it. I don't care for what they say. I only hate the indecency of showing them what I have loved'.

But Carrington was caught in a trap of her own making, by refusing to exhibit she was placed somewhere in between an amateur and a professional painter. As usual, she was her own sternest critic, acutely aware of possible failings: 'I think Simon's [Bussy] remark that there was something more in my work than a student's, comforts me more than anything. So often I fear that after all I am just what I was at the Slade, a promising student with some skill, and even if there is only a little grain of the other, as long as someone like Simon sees it, it gives one confidence in oneself. For I care so much.'

That she lacked a foothold in the contemporary art scene was also something she was well aware of. In 1920 she painted a portrait of Lady Strachey, Lytton's mother, and afterwards wrote to Alix Strachey, 'The painters of Gordon Square rather sniff at the picture. I see I shall never fit in any "school". I am not modern enough for the French style, and too clumsy to be a New Englisher.' While it is true that Carrington's work was not modernist enough to attract critical kudos, it was anything but clumsy and by rights belongs in a tradition of fellow English painters such as Augustus John, Gwen John, Henry Lamb, Nina Hamnett, Spencer Gore, and Harold Gilman. That she has been neglected – at least as an artist – is due to a combination of factors: her own diffidence and reluctance to exhibit, conventional sexism which denigrates women's achievements, and the historiography of Bloomsbury which, until recently, has esteemed its literary achievements at the expense of its visual artists. To this should be added the conflicts of Carrington's personal life which illustrate some of the pressures – external and internal – which impede women's progress and prevent them from achieving their full potential.

Life and Art – A Marriage or Divorce?

When Carrington chose to live with Lytton and move away from London, it was more than a physical change of location. She did, possibly with conscious deliberation, cut herself off from the solidly middle-class and 'ordinary' values of her family background, and embraced the more radical values of Bloomsbury. 'Bloomsbury' has become associated with bohemian relationships and liberal beliefs, but it was also a lifestyle based on inherited wealth and upper-middle class privilege. The necessity of material comforts provided by the work of servants was taken for granted. There is a sense that once Carrington entered that life she was reluctant to leave its cocooned sensibilities and her letters are noticeably devoid of reference to what was happening in the outside world. Yet she herself inhabited an ambivalent position in relationship to Strachey and his friends.

Reading Carrington's letters to Lytton, and his to her, two things are very clear. Firstly that she loved him passionately and deeply; throughout the correspondence covering the sixteen years they spent together, she constantly reiterates her love for him, and her feelings were those of a *lover*, not a close friend. But his feelings were more detached. He was clearly fond of Carrington, and at times writes of his appreciation of her role in his life, with respect and gratitude. Beyond that however, he was not prepared to go. With Carrington looking after his domestic welfare and providing the setting for pleasant and sociable Bloomsbury weekends, he was free to come and go; Tidmarsh and Ham Spray may have been his base, but they were not his whole life.

On his death-bed, Strachey expressed a regret that he hadn't married Carrington. He obviously *could* have married her – it certainly wasn't unknown for homosexual men to marry – if only to maintain a respectable front, and Strachey had earlier considered proposing to Virginia Woolf (before she married Leonard Woolf). The likely truth of the matter is that he did not consider Carrington his social equal. She was keenly aware of the inadequacies of her girlhood education and embarked on a process of self-education; part of Strachey's attraction was his erudite and critically acute mind. When alone together their companionship was marked by a close accord, Lytton's idiosyncratic wit and love of the absurd, colluding with Carrington's extravagant imagination and inventive sense of humour. But ultimately Strachey's loyalty was to the Cambridge-educated, male, very literary hegemony of Bloomsbury, and Carrington was relegated to second place.

Nevertheless, Carrington, with great perseverance held together their tenuous arrangement and ultimately their relationship achieved a harmony and stability which seemed to suit them both. Certainly Carrington benefited in several significant ways important to an artist – she had financial security and time to herself. While Strachey may not have been actively encouraging to Carrington in her work, neither was he completely oblivious to, or unsupportive of her talents; when they were living at Ham Spray, he had a studio built especially for Carrington to work in. Paradoxically, it was Carrington's relationship with Strachey that gave her the freedom she wanted, and this was part of his attraction for her. As Frances Partridge has observed[15], it was 'no accident that she concentrated her most intense love on someone who made no emotional demands on her, and was thus in a sense unattainable – Lytton'. Although Carrington was attracted to other men – notably Ralph Partridge (whom she married) and Gerald Brenan[16] – she felt stifled and trapped by their possessive demands and was reluctant to fully commit herself. Lytton Strachey's sexuality provided a built-in detachment which she clearly found less oppressive. But the question remains: at what cost to herself and to her self-esteem did she perform the delicate balancing act that constituted her relationship with Strachey?

Divisions and Dichotomies

From the perspective of the 1980s one can see that Carrington's life story characterizes a lot of specifically feminine contradictions which had their effect on her career as an artist. In particular she was at the mercy of certain emotional and social obligations which have always placed a heavy burden on women, and prevented them 'achieving' in the same way as men. In her autobiography, *Drawn From Life*, the painter Stella Bowen[17] identifies this problem in describing the pitfalls of what she calls 'female devotion':

> Any artist knows, that after a good bout of work one is both too tired and too excited to be of any use to anyone. To be obliged to tackle other people's problems, or merely to cook their meals, the moment one lays down pen or brush, is intolerably hard. What one wants, on the contrary, is for other people to occupy themselves with one's own moods and requirements; to lie on a sofa and listen to music, and have things brought to one on a tray! That is why a man writer or painter always manages to get some woman to look after him and make his life easy.... A professional woman, however, seldom gets this cushioning unless she can pay for it.

In Carrington's relationship with Lytton Strachey, she was clearly the one who 'brought him things on a tray' and made sure the household was running smoothly for his benefit; her own work as a painter was unlikely to have been considered as important as his as a writer. The necessity to sell her work or seek critical recognition would not have been considered a *priority*. It is easy to see how Carrington's artistic talents were seen as essentially decorative, feminine, and peripheral, and she herself characterised as an appendage to a More Important Man.

Typically, Carrington could readily identify and pinpoint the problem of having divided commitments: in a letter to Alix Strachey[18] she describes how

> Lytton is very busy now on proofs of Victoria and publishers, but I must say considering he isn't writing, he seems to spend his entire day with 'acquaintances'. I suppose the obvious retort is that after two years hermitage, he wants diversion, still the fact remains that I only saw him two days this week and those times only by dint of ruining my entire day. By galavanting off at absurd hours to meet him. I am an idiot Alix to complain. Because really I might be so much worse off. Still its that old business we used to discuss, of the difficulty of concentrating when one has one ear on the telephone, or an eye out of the window.

Although she enjoyed creating a home for him she was not unaware of the inequalities of her situation[19]: 'a sort of overboiling seizes me sometimes when I am interrupted in my studio to turn off the water and have to put logs on the fires and order all these meals, and to hear these perpetual shrieks in the sitting room and nobody stirring a finger to do any work in the house'.

Carrington herself, in her letters and diaries, provides a clear analysis of the contradictions between 'being an artist' and 'being a woman' with all that the latter implies in terms of social obligations and sexual expectations. She never found a satisfactory way of resolving these conflicts for herself, and her commitments were always divided between her own work and the needs of others. Tragically, in her case, this syndrome was compounded by internalized feelings of failure and dissatisfaction, a fundamental and debilitating lack of belief in herself:

> You know I think it's very difficult to live quite by myself. I keep on pretending I am GOD but it all seems rather a deception ... I can't quite make myself do anything for myself, eating seems tiresome, and one lies in a chair dreaming of colours, and pulling out visions, instead of eating tea ... I wonder if it is a fundamental difference between female and male – this GOD business and one's

disinterestness in oneself[20].

Carrington 'lacked' the single-minded determination and
masculine certainty that would have led to greater achievement *and*
recognition as an artist. She poured so much of her herself into her love
for Lytton, there was little left for herself. After his death she wrote in
her diary: 'I feel as if I was in a dream almost unconscious, so much of me
was in you.' For her it was Lytton who brought harmony and stability
into her life, giving it a shape and a meaning, and without him there
seemed little point to her life. It seems now more likely that the reverse is
true – that it was she who brought order and security into his life – but
she was unable to value it on those terms.

Carrington killed herself after Lytton died and conventionally it is
said that she did this because she couldn't bear to go on living without
him. No doubt this is partly true; but it would also be true to say that her
death was the result – expressed in a particularly melodramatic way – of
conflicts and dilemmas familiar to many women. It is the final irony of
her life that she could be, in many ways, so independent and yet
dependent on a man who could not – in the conventional sense – return
her love. Like many women, Carrington lived out her creative and
emotional life through another person, and it cost her her life.

The Creative Canvas

Although Carrington had contradictory and complex feelings about
'being a woman', she was drawn to her own sex and her women friends
were important to her. 'But Alix I miss you badly and often wish
sometimes you had been a sappho, we might have had such a happy life
without these Strachey's!'[21], she writes to Alix Strachey (who was married
to Lytton's brother James). She did in fact have several lesbian
relationships which she evidently found far less problematic than her
sexual affairs with men.

Carrington is interesting as a modern heroine precisely because she
didn't fit into conventional roles – or rather she fitted in in a misfit kind
of way; she married but didn't want to be married, disliked femininity yet
put a great regard on her female friendships, was attracted to lesbianism
but maintained a kind of bisexuality, and loved a man who would have
preferred her to be a boy.

Carrington put a lot of energy and time into maintaining her
friendships, just as she expended a great deal of emotional commitment
on creating a home for Lytton and entertaining his friends. Such
achievements are seen as 'feminine' attributes and are not socially
endorsed in the same way as the masculine prerogatives of running a

LARREAU
SNOWSCAPE
1922

—

OIL ON CANVAS
30.48×40.64cm
PRIVATE COLLECTION

THE FEET BATHING
PARTY
1919

—

WATERCOLOUR
43.18×35.56cm
PRIVATE COLLECTION

business and using managerial skills. Carrington is a classic case of a woman artist whose talents and achievements have been undervalued precisely because they were associated with a definition of feminine creativity as small-scale, domestic, and decorative. In fact, the emphasis should be placed the other way round: Carrington took forms of domestic art and did something quite extraordinary and unique with them. After her death, Julia Strachey wrote an appreciation of Carrington which pays tribute to her particular style as a person and the way her creativity was intrinsic to her sexuality:

> Emotional herself, though she was afraid of others depending on her emotionally, she had an immense richness and range of feeling: was a productive creator, showering jokes, elegancies, and perceptiveness wherever she went, possessing a great gift for 'seeing the point' of another person's wit or style. A lot of her qualities were essentially feminine – her sly teasingness, her lightness of touch, the fact that her whole life was a creation in fire, feeling, and style: her lack of knowledge and education also and the remarkable impression of sunlight she made.'[22]

Her work, in all its diversity, is the product of a creativity that found its expression in forms more ingenious, imaginative, and intriguing than the more orthodox parameters of what is usually perceived and understood as art. During her short life, she produced a body of work which both stands up to traditional art criticism and goes beyond it.

WINIFRED
NICHOLSON
1893-1981

'Colour is one of the surest means
of expressing joy...'

In 1954, when she was sixty-one, Winifred Nicholson wrote an article
entitled 'I like to have a Picture in my Room'. In this she explained to her
readers how an original painting was a vital component of the ingredients
of her ideal room. She did not state that it had to be one of her own
works, but her description of the type of painting she was prepared to
hang on her wall reveals her ideas about the purpose of art:

> Pictures have played many roles. They have been altar-pieces,
> fetishes, idols, the courtly decorations of palaces, the flattery of
> princes, historical records, vain fancies and vain fables. I want
> none of these pictures. I have no place for them in my home. My
> dwelling room has too much going on in it for such extravagant
> luxuries. In the morning it is a sanctuary, in the daytime a factory,
> in the evening a place of festivity, and through the night a place of
> rest. I want a window in it, I want a telephone, a radio and a
> television set. All these are contacts and doors into the outer
> world. But besides these, and more than all these, I want a focal
> point, something alive and silent....So the picture...must be an
> anchor for security, must be a lamp for delight, must be a well of
> peace...

For Winifred Nicholson the significant nature of a picture can be
inferred from the final sentence where it is listed as an anchor, a lamp and
a well of peace. She gives no clue as to what the picture should depict;
however her own work reveals that flowers come top of the list of
subjects to paint. Flowers were very important to her because she
believed that they held the key to an understanding of the phenomenal
world around us all. Winifred Nicholson could be classified as a painter of
flowers, since they were her principal subject throughout her life. But, for
her, flower painting was no simple matter. She did not paint flowers just
because they were there. Neither did she paint them because she thought
they would sell well. She painted them because for her they captured and
reflected qualities of light, and therefore of *life*.

The painting of flowers however, is not seen to be at the cutting
edge of what constitutes the modern in modern art and because Winifred

WINIFRED NICHOLSON
in the 1920's
—

WINIFRED AND
BEN NICHOLSON
AND TUFTY,
CUMBERLAND
C.1924
—
COURTESY OF
JAKE NICHOLSON

WINIFRED ROBERTS
(AFTERWARDS
NICHOLSON) ON
HOLIDAY, TIPPACOT,
DEVON
1920
—
COURTESY OF
JAKE NICHOLSON

Nicholson was quite content to keep to flower subjects or related topics all her working life, her career has not been one that has kept her in the forefront of avant-garde art in Britain in the twentieth century. Nevertheless, for just over a decade, from the mid-1920s to the start of the Second World War, she enjoyed a generous measure of fame and success in the London art world. She had four large solo exhibitions of paintings in major London commercial galleries between 1925 and 1936, all of which were well received critically and from which the majority of the works were sold.

This period of fame coincided with her working partnership with the painter Ben Nicholson, her husband from 1920 until the early 1930s when he went to live with the sculptor Barbara Hepworth. The break-up of their marriage was not something that Winifred found easy to come to terms with or to reconcile with her feelings for Ben (she did not re-marry), and it is an indication of her generous spirit that she maintained a close friendship with him. Her relationship with Ben Nicholson did not cease when they no longer lived together; it lasted the whole of their long lives and was a support to them both. In 1987 a book entitled *Unknown Colour*, which contained her writings as well as her paintings, was published and this revealed a fascinating exchange of letters between Winifred and Ben Nicholson in which they encourage and criticize each others' work.

As Ben Nicholson's career grew in international stature from the 1940s onwards, Winifred Nicholson appears to have allowed hers to assume a quieter role. At one point in the early 1930s, when they were both achieving recognition as prominent members of the modern movement in British art, he appears to have suggested to her that she change her name so that there would not be confusion over two artists with the same name producing similar kinds of work. She concurred with this though it is interesting that she did not use her maiden name of Roberts, but instead took on a name that was of historical significance for her family, Dacre. (The Dacres of Gisland in Cumbria were her ancestors.) She used this surname from the early 1930s until the end of the Second World War and then reverted back to Nicholson even though she was by then divorced.

This could be viewed in the light of a self-effacing traditionally feminine reflex, and that was no doubt in part involved in Nicholson's response. But it is also the case that she did not *need* fame. She had financial security throughout her life and didn't therefore have an imperative need to make a lot of money from her work, but just as importantly, she was secure in herself - a balanced, self-contained person who was totally committed to her work and professional in her approach. She knew what she wanted to achieve in her work and did not require the approbation of the outside world. So although Winifred Nicholson was not particularly concerned with being a famous artist, or in selling her paintings for high prices, neither did she have any false modesty about her talent. She knew she was good and she probably realized that her work – and her theories about colour – would be more appreciated after her death than in her lifetime. Some pioneering abstract paintings which she had executed in Paris in the 1930s were rediscovered in the mid-1970s and this served, late in her life, to give a fresh outlook on her artistic career. Before her death in 1981, she was aware that preparations were underway for a major retrospective of her work to be held at the Tate Gallery in 1987, and this afforded her much pleasure.

In 1979 she began to plan the writing of a book about colour theory, which she was going to title *The Scale of the Rainbow.* As she died before this could be accomplished, instead her family have published *Unknown Colour,* a collection of her writings and paintings, compiled by her son Andrew Nicholson. This has proved to be a rich source for an understanding of her paintings. Winifred Nicholson wrote fluently and with a freshness and originality that is mirrored in her pictures.

Influences

Winifred Nicholson was born in 1893, the eldest daughter of Charles and Lady Cecilia Roberts. Her father, the son of an Anglican clergyman, had an active political career while her mother was an amateur painter and a member of the aristocratic Howard family. Since the sixteenth century the Howards had owned large areas of land in Yorkshire and Cumbria and had built Castle Howard in Yorkshire and extended the medieval Naworth Castle in Cumbria. Thus from her early days, Winifred Nicholson was used to staying in grand country houses surrounded by servants, and this aspect of her family background played its part in the formation of her character. Her maternal grandmother was Rosalind Howard, Countess of Carlisle, who was known as the 'Radical Countess' on account of the causes for which she campaigned, such as Liberalism, Women's Suffrage and Temperance. Her energy in promoting the latter cause brought about the closure of all the inns and public houses in and around Brampton in Cumbria. Nicholson inherited much of the Countess of Carlisle's reforming zeal, formidable energy and enjoyment of life. It was also through her mother's family that Winifred was introduced into an artistic environment. Her mother and her grandfather, George Howard, the ninth Earl of Carlisle, encouraged her to paint from nature, using the landscapes and flowers found on the family estates.

Flowers began to fascinate her as a little girl. She kept nature notebooks recording the varieties of wild flowers around her parents' home at Bracklands in Surrey, and on her grandfather's country estate at Naworth Castle. She expressed her gratitude for wild flowers everywhere 'who have blossomed before my eyes and inspired me, whether they knew it or whether they did not.' Flowers, to her, 'were the secret of the cosmos' with their 'roots…in the dark earth' and their 'flowerface seeing the brightness of the sun, a brightness that is too bright to see.' A flower was therefore the most simple and direct link between the earth and the sun, and a reconciler of opposites. Flowers were also valuable and inspirational to Nicholson because they offered a vast range of colours. She believed that the purest colour on earth was to be found in the petals of flowers, especially wild flowers, and in jewels. Having no interest in precious stones, Nicholson concentrated her artistic attention upon the hues of flowers. A painting for her would be constructed not by its arrangement of forms, but by its colour harmonies; this became a crucial cornerstone of her working practice.

Her response to flowers was not confined to that of colour interest only. She believed that flowers told their 'stories' to those who were willing to listen and that their message could be transmitted via paint or by prose. In 1976 she published a book called *Flower Tales,* in which seven stories, some with the titles 'Morning Dew', 'The Flower Show', 'The Bells of Elfland', were interspersed with illustrations of her flower paintings. Her *Flower Tales* continue the genre of Hans Christian Anderson's tales, like *The Snow Queen* in which the flowers tell their stories to Little Gerda.

On looking back over her career from the vantage point of the 1970s Winifred Nicholson recorded that she had started as a painter of 'faerie' pictures. She learnt to be a painter, first at home with her grandfather, George Howard, 9th Earl of Carlisle, and then at the Byam Shaw School of Art, London. Her grandfather was self-taught and a great friend of many of the Pre-Raphaelite painters, such as Edward Burne-Jones and William Morris. He had also enjoyed a fruitful working relationship with an Italian painter, Giovanni Costa, founder of the so-called Etruscan School which specialized in landscapes and architecture-scapes, presenting the natural world as though it was Arcadian, that is, a place of rustic paradise. John Byam Shaw, the founder of the art school with his name, painted pictures which display a delicate sensibility and a stress on the poetic imagination for their subject matter. Thus Winifred Nicholson's early training as an artist was in the Pre-Raphaelite mode (what she meant by 'faerie' pictures); that is she learnt to draw and paint directly from nature; her own imaginative compositions would have laid great stress upon a poetic vision and a sense of escapism from the everyday urban world.

Nicholson studied at the Byam Shaw School until the age of

twenty-six, and her artistic practice could have continued to rely upon the technique of careful delineation of detail and choice of symbolic subjects preferred by Byam Shaw and his circle. However, just at this moment, she was lucky enough to have her horizons greatly expanded. Her father, Charles Roberts, a Member of Parliament and Under-Secretary of State for India, was sent to India on a long fact-finding tour. Winifred and her sister Christina accompanied their father. In India Winifred Nicholson not only learned to open her mind to Eastern religious thought, but her eyes were excited by the strong light, bright colours and sharp tonal distinctions of the Indian scene. In India she 'noticed how eastern art uses lilac to create sunlight,'[1] and this discovery led her to experiment with the colour violet. On her return to England this caused her work to become bolder and more individual. She had found her own unique colouristic way of breaking free from the patterns of thought inculcated at art school.

Winifred and Ben Nicholson

At this exciting stage in her life, she met and fell in love with Ben Nicholson, also a painter and a year younger than herself. He was the son of the painters Sir William Nicholson and Mabel Pryde. His early work was influenced by the sombre low-key colour range preferred by his parents, and his chosen subject matter was studio-based punctiliously placed still-lifes, showing something of the influence of the Cubists and of Cézanne. Ben Nicholson had spent most of the years of the First World War outside Britain, partly in Madeira and California for health reasons, and when he returned to London in the winter of 1918 he was unsure whether to make painting his career. Winifred's already marked dedication as a painter would have provided him with an impressive model. The great benefit of the marriage of these two young painters in 1920 was that each brought a new approach to the other's art and working practices.

At the beginning of their marriage Ben and Winifred Nicholson lived partly in rented accommodation in London and partly at the Villa Capriccio, a house perched on a steep hillside outside the village of Castagnola, above Lake Lugano in Switzerland. The Villa Capriccio was bought for Winifred by her father, who travelled out from England to complete the purchase. Winifred Nicholson was able to call on family money when necessary at the beginning of her married life, whereas Ben Nicholson had more limited financial back-up.

Ben and Winifred painted in a rented studio in the King's Road when in London, and in two separate rooms in their mountain villa when in Switzerland. After 1924, when Winifred Nicholson bought a house on land near to the family estates in Cumbria, they both had separate studios

VILLA CARPRICCIO,
LUGANO, TICINO,
SWITZERLAND; BEN
AND WINIFRED
NICHOLSON'S HOME IN
THE EARLY
1920's

———

JAKE NICHOLSON

FIRE AND WATER
1927
———
OIL ON CANVAS
68×56cm
ARTIST'S FAMILY

BEN AND JAKE
1927
—
OIL ON CANVAS
74×59cm
ARTIST'S FAMILY

JAKE AND KATE ON THE
ISLE OF WIGHT
1931-2
—
OIL ON CANVAS
67.3×74.9cm
CITY OF BRISTOL
MUSEUM AND ART
GALLERY

on the first floor of this house. It was a seventeenth-century stone farmhouse called Bankshead, built on top of a milecastle on Hadrian's wall, the Roman wall which divided Cumberland from the Scottish lowlands and Winifred Nicholson lived there from 1924 until her death in 1981. She extended the farmhouse garden, planted a larch wood to keep the east winds at bay, and established an informal mixture of wild and garden plants, which served as subjects for her paintings. Although she had a first floor room which was designated her studio, Nicholson was also capable of painting on top of the kitchen table once the breakfast things were cleared, or using the back of a domestic chair as an easel. Her favourite room for painting was her bedroom, with her working space set in front of the window, through which she could see a view of the Cumbrian foothills of the Pennines, Cold Fell and Tindale Fell in the distance and her own garden close at hand.

Ben Nicholson, according to Winifred's reminiscences, consciously made his painting activity into a highly professional job, transcending domestic responsibilities with no difficulty. She, on the other hand, had either to cook lunch and supper in a house with no gas and electricity, or to organize a housemaid or local helper to do it for her. Winifred Nicholson's daily routine in the 1920s was to a large extent dominated by the large black range in the front living room at Bankshead. As if to underline this aspect of her existence, she painted a handful of pictures that included this range, FIRE AND WATER being one of these. She also wrote about it:

> Bankshead altar was its hearth. Within its thick stone walls its fire held its comfort, its glow, its warmth – the fireplace was an open one with an oven to one side and a tank to hold water on the other, an arm to hang a kettle over the open blaze – on this I cooked with joy.

Nicholson enjoyed her marriage and domesticity, and valued the creative potential in home-making, cooking, gardening and dress-making. She viewed marriage as 'sacred', and fulfilled her roles as wife, daughter, mother and eventually grandmother, with energy and enthusiasm. She found the dual careers of being a painter and a mother complementary, though was not always able to accomplish such a reconciliation without a struggle. She wrote about 'life' and 'art' sometimes pulling in different directions, but if you can achieve a harmony between them, 'the two dragons become friends and helpmates'.

Nicholson experienced some gynaecological problems, and for many years thought that she was unable to have children. Then, when she did conceive and was seven months pregnant with her first child she suffered a fall and badly injured her back. She placed great confidence in children's way of making sense of things, feeling that they generally 'got it right'. Winifred Nicholson is not generally known as a painter of figure compositions or portraits, but she did paint a number of pictures celebrating her marriage, her husband and the birth and growth of her three children. See for example BEN AND JAKE, and JAKE AND KATE ON THE ISLE OF WIGHT , which illustrate the way in which she was able to combine 'life' and 'art', making one a fulfilment of the other.

Winifred Nicholson became a Christian Scientist in the late 1920s, and her children believe that for her part of the attraction of Christian Science was due to it being a relatively new religious movement – it was founded in the USA in the 1880s – and having a woman, Mary Baker Eddy, as its charismatic founder and leader. The teachings of Christian Science put forward a belief in the dominance of Mind or Spirit over matter. Matter is seen not as a God-created substance, but as a limited mode of human perception which it is possible to transcend through spiritual belief. Nicholson clearly put her beliefs to work in her attitude to painting and this clarifies why she was so interested in testing the limits of perception, particularly in questions of light and colour.

She combined this spiritual approach with an extremely pragmatic attitude to the painting of a picture. Interviewed late in life about how to make a painting Winifred Nicholson replied: 'You set out your colours and you start to paint and you don't stop until you've finished.' She liked to work fast, and where possible, to complete a painting in one sitting, an approach which required total absorption and concentration. Nicholson exercised critical judgement on her own work by the simple expedient of re-using a painting that she felt had not worked by turning the canvas over on the stretcher and starting again on the other side. Quite a large proportion of her paintings throughout her career have a picture on both sides of the canvas. Some are reprimed with a white ground, and a new picture sits on top of an older abandoned one.

Flowers on a window-sill

When Winifred Nicholson showed twenty-seven works, mostly flower paintings, at an exhibition at a London gallery shared with Ben Nicholson in May 1923, Frank Rutter, a respected critic, stated that she was the inventor of a new kind of flowerpiece, and in this he was quite correct. It appears that Winifred Nicholson, in the early 1920s, was the first artist to paint a bunch of flowers in a vase or jar set on a window-sill before a beautiful, rolling, extensive landscape without putting in the window or the middle ground. She gives the viewer foreground and background but the 'in between' element is diffused. She thus reconciles and balances the near and the far in these flower paintings. Paintings such as CANDLEMASS I,

GOBLET AND TWO
PEARS BY BEN
NICHOLSON
c.1927

—

OIL ON BOARD
35.6×43.2cm
KETTLE'S YARD,
CAMBRIDGE

JULIA STRACHEY
—
OIL ON CANVAS
38×45.72cm
PRIVATE COLLECTION

THE MILL AT
TIDMARSH
BERKSHIRE
1918
—
OIL ON CANVAS
71.1 × 101.6cm
PRIVATE COLLECTION

TILES FOR FIREPLACE
SURROUND
1930
—
14 CERAMIC PAINTED
TILES
OVERALL SIZE
76.2×77.5cm
THE ANTHONY
D'OFFAY GALLERY
LONDON

MUGHETTI
1921
—
OIL ON BOARD
54×58cm
PRIVATE COLLECTION

SPANISH WOMAN
DATE UNKNOWN
—
SILVER FOIL
OIL AND INK
25.4×30.48cm
GIVEN TO DORELIA JOHN
BY CARRINGTON
AND FOR MANY YEARS
HUNG AT FRYERN
COURT
PRIVATE COLLECTION

BLUE HEPTAGONS

1936

———

OIL ON BOARD

49.5×75cm

THE ARTIST'S FAMILY

HONEYSUCKLE AND

SWEETPEAS

1950

———

OIL ON BOARD

44×71.7cm

ABERDEEN ART

GALLERY

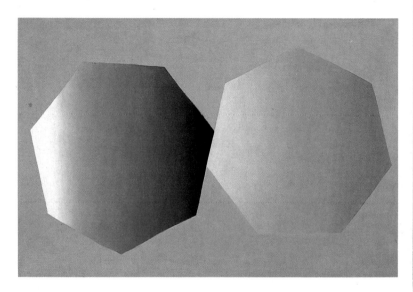

Winifred Nicholson

COPPER AND CAPARI

1967

——

OIL ON CANVAS

59.7 × 59.7 cm

PRIVATE COLLECTION

LIVE PEWTER and MOONLIGHT, POTS LOAN extend this theme to explore a
way of constructing a sense of mystery and wonder between small, living
growing thing, and the larger horizon to which they relate. The critic
Christopher Neve describes this particular skill of Nicholson's:

> Often her most memorable paintings include tender, budding
> flowers in the foreground with a luminous depth beyond,
> culminating in a rhythmic horizon of fells. Her subject became
> flowers and space, the flowers like sparks of pure colour against a
> mysterious radiance in which the eye is free to focus back and
> forth.[2]

This central theme of Nicholson's work became a means of
pushing out the boundaries of what painting could achieve, which for her
was, 'the point where painting touches "spiritual reality" – the
fundamental essence of things, beneath, behind, beyond, and before,
visual experience[3]'. This 'spiritual reality' was not found in the appearance
of things, but in what Nicholson called the 'true juxtaposition or
relationship' *between* things. It is not necessary to know about
Nicholson's spiritual beliefs to understand her *œuvre*, (one of the
strengths of her work is its accessibility), but an appreciation of what she
brought to her painting and the resonance of her images, adds a further
level of meaning.

Nicholson was particularly fond of placing her bunch of flowers in
a glass container and of painting this bunch set before a landscape which
consisted mainly of a large expanse of water. Many of the windows at her
Swiss mountain home afforded views of the blue waters of Lake Lugano,
and later in her life, she rented remote cottages on Scottish islands
through the windows of which she could again look out on to ever-
changing patterns of waves and light. Nicholson was aware that glass and
water act as diffusers of light, causing rays of light to be broken up. She
was very interested in light because of its relationship to colour; light
makes colour visible and colour dies when light dies. She was also
fascinated by rainbows and prisms, because they both split light into its
component parts, into the spectrum of seven colours – red, orange,
yellow, blue, indigo and violet – the bands of which make up a rainbow's
arch or a prism's ray. She used an evocative phrase to describe how a glass
container placed in front of a sheet of water made the light break up and
its beams become tossed to and fro 'like a shuttlecock'. This reminds the
viewer how she made her pictures work; our eyes go back and forth
across the wide expanses of space and return to the focal point of the
composition, the bunch of flowers on the window-sill.

In 1922 Winifred Nicholson painted a pot of lilies of the valley on

CYCLAMEN AND
PRIMULA
c.1922
—
OIL ON BOARD
49.2×54.6cm
KETTLE'S YARD,
CAMBRIDGE

POLYANTHUS AND
CINERARIA
1921
—
OIL ON CANVAS
51×59cm
PRIVATE COLLECTION

BANKSHEAD: THE
NICHOLSONS' HOME –
IN THE EARLY
1920's
—
ARTIST'S FAMILY

LIVE PEWTER
1959
—
OIL ON BOARD
60×76.2cm
PRIVATE COLLECTION

P.133 the window-sill of her villa above Lake Lugano. The painting is called Mughetti because that is the Italian word for lily of the valley, and it shows the pot of living flowers still wrapped in white tissue paper from the florists. She used this idea again in other paintings, for example Polyanthus and Cineraria, retaining the paper wrapper because its whiteness served to intensify the colours of the flowers against which it was set. Nicholson often referred to Mughetti in her writings and her letters, believing it to be one of her best works and the first painting of her maturity. It also personified for her an important quality of emotion, that of love, because of the way the paper enfolds and embraces the delicate flowers. Two examples are pertinent: 'Ben had given me a pot of lilies of the valley, Mughetti, in a tissue paper wrapper – this I stood on the window-sill, behind was azure blue, mountain, lake, sky, all there, and the tissue paper wrapper held the secret of the universe[4]' and 'The idea of marriage I had when we married is expressed in Mughetti. I remember thinking of it while I painted. Love and the secret lovely things that it unfolds.[5]'

In 1958, in a letter to her friend, the poet Kathleen Raine, Winifred Nicholson revealed that thus far in her life, she had had three moments of especial significance for her life and her painting. She called these moments 'a glimpse through' and if they could be defined they could be seen as distinctive moments of light. The three times when she felt she had had 'a glimpse through' were her painting spell at the Villa Capriccio, which culminated in the painting Mughetti, her time in Paris in the 1930s and a time with Kathleen Raine, painting on the Scottish island of Eigg in the 1950s. Nicholson loved painting on the remote Scottish islands of South Uist, Skye, Canna, (see Isle of Canna, 1951), Rhum and Eigg (her last painting holiday, at the age of eighty-six, was taken on the island of Eigg) because of the quality of the cool silvery light found there.

She also liked to travel abroad in order to find a different quality of light and a different range of colours. In the 1960s she went on painting trips to Greece and North Africa with her artist daughter, Kate, where she encountered a brighter range of light than in Switzerland, Cumberland or Scotland, and also brighter colours and stronger tonal P.136 contrasts. The painting Copper and Capari (1967) is a striking example of her use of a brighter range of colours, and it keeps to her favourite theme of flowers on a window-sill. The window-sill is that of Winifred Nicholson's hotel room (and makeshift studio) at the Belle Hélène Hotel overlooking Mycenae in Greece. She set the copper jug, on the left of the sill, against the red-brown earth colour of the Greek mountain behind, obviously enjoying the colour and spatial relationship between the two. The mountain becomes bluer, or more violet in colour, as it recedes and this colour is picked up in the sky above. It is also used as part of the

Winifred Nicholson

ISLE OF CANNA
1951
—
OIL ON CANVAS
63.5×76.2cm
PRIVATE COLLECTION

shadows in the sunlit glass containers on the window-sill in the foreground. The two white flowers in both the copper jug and the glass in the centre are caper flowers (Capparis Spinosa) and they provide the 'capari' part of the picture's title.

P.135   Honeysuckle and Sweetpeas (circa 1945-6), which is one of the most popular paintings in the collection of Aberdeen Art Gallery, is a painting of two bunches of variegated flowers in plain vases. Although it is perhaps the most well-known of Winifred Nicholson's paintings, probably because it has been in a public collection and on public view since 1950, it is rather unusual because the vases of flowers are not set on a window-sill. Instead they are placed on a curved table top in an undifferentiated space. Nicholson wrote that she wished to paint pictures that 'call down colour, so that a picture can be a lamp in one's home, not merely a window[6]'. Honeysuckle and Sweetpeas is a marvellous example of Winifred Nicholson's ability to create luminosity; it is not just a representation of two vases containing flowers but also a magical picture that seems to emit both light and colour. It has a radiant quality which is characteristic of Winifred Nicholson's work in general. Although the framework of the painting is quite formal, with both vases of the same size set along the same axis, there is a mood of great tenderness and communion between the flowers in the vases. The tendrils in the vase on the left appear to want to reach out and touch the flowers in the neighbouring vase. Like Mughetti it is a painting that offers an emotional charge. It is equally charged with saturated colour, with a range of yellows heightened by the addition of Winifred Nicholson's favourite tint of violet.

In an unpublished article written in the 1960s – *Artists as Women* – Winifred Nicholson reserves her highest praise for the flower paintings of the women artists who were part of the court circle of the Chinese Emperors. These courtly women artists – Lady Khan, Chung-chi, Ma Hsung-har, Hsiche, Susu, Yango and Lady Li – produced works 'that can easily be distinguished from those of the men artists because of their divine quality which in Chinese is called 'shen' quality. No man artist has painted 'shen' that I know of. It is this 'shen' quality that we now need. What is it? It cannot be put into words. But if one had to – I would use the word wonder, great wonder.' Nicholson does not include herself along with these Chinese women artists as a creator of works with 'shen' quality, but there is no doubt that her best work is imbued with just this essence and radiance.

Winifred Nicholson

Paris Light

When, in the autumn of 1931, Ben Nicholson decided to live in London with Barbara Hepworth, Winifred Nicholson had to consider carefully where she was to live, along with her three young children, Andrew the youngest being only a couple of months old. She felt that she did not want to remain all the year in Cumbria and could not cope with living in London, so she found rented accommodation in Cornwall and the Isle of Wight until the autumn of 1932, when she bravely took herself, her three small children and a nursemaid off to Paris. Several pictures exist from the Cornish and Isle of Wight periods, for example JAKE AND KATE ON THE ISLE OF WIGHT which testify to Nicholson's commitment to painting even when her private life was under severe stress. Her son Jake believes that she decided to move to Paris because she felt that it was at that time the most exciting place for artists and for aesthetic experimentation.

From 1933 until September 1938 Winifred Nicholson, with her three children and Cissy the nursemaid, lived in a third floor flat overlooking the river Seine at 48 Quai d'Auteuil, Paris. She had one of the front rooms which overlooked the river as her bedroom and studio and she worked there in her usual manner, with her current picture propped up on the back of a chair instead of using an easel. What she particularly valued about her flat was its view over the Seine. Directly opposite, on the left bank, was a modern Citroen factory and at night this was brightly lit. The factory lights, along with the lights of the numerous barges, were reflected on the ceiling of her room. Nicholson's painting PARIS LIGHT (circa 1933-4) records her interest in reflected light and prismatic colour. The picture presents a section of the ceiling of the sitting room in her Paris flat and on it, along with the hanging light bulb, are a series of little rainbows and a white square with a grey vase shape set within. The marks on the ceiling are caused by the light on a sunny day bouncing off the surface of the river, entering the sitting room at an angle via the window and shining through a modern square glass table on which Nicholson had placed a vase of flowers. This table with its vase of flowers casts a strange negative/positive shadow on the ceiling while the little rainbows are formed by the light striking the edges of the glass table and splitting up into its seven component bands of colour. PARIS LIGHT is an unusual painting, which at first glance looks like an abstract picture. This is not surprising because circa 1934-5, shortly after the painting of this work, Nicholson produced a series of abstract pictures.

She experimented with abstract art partly because of her great interest in colour and partly because other avant-garde artists in Paris were also travelling the same path. She became a friend of many of the most important artists then working in Paris, Piet Mondrian, Constantin

Brancusi, Cézar Domela, Jean Helion, Naum Gabo, Alberto Giacometti.
She bought very new work by Mondrian, Helion, Gabo and Giacometti,
probably before any other British artist had done so and wrote of her
time then: 'These were years of inspiration – fizzing like a soda water
bottle....Boundaries and barriers were broken down....We talked in the
cafés of the new vision, the new scale of music, the new architecture –
unnecessary things were to be done away with and art was to be
functional.[7]' Paris represented a sense of freedom for Nicholson, and this
experimentation consolidated her theories about the freedom of colour.
She felt that colours are free. She wrote how 'colours are, to many people,
connected with known objects, for example green with grass and red with
letter boxes.' But she wanted the viewer to feel instead that colours were
'halts in the river of light' (another of her simple, yet poetic phrases).
'The Old Masters', she wrote, 'nailed colour like a carpet tight down over
forms', while she wished to release colour from this subservient role and
allow it to speak first and foremost for itself. She felt that colour should
not necessarily be confined by shapes and she was always looking for a
way in which the shapes should be bounded by the colour rather than the
other way round.

Recalling her time in Paris in the mid 1930s, Winifred Nicholson
wrote that 'then I had discarded all my Pre-Raphaelite romance – copying
the visual world of appearance – and with fond delight traced with a
compass and set square proportions that leapt out of the canvas
unexpected to my thought and to my eye[8].' Nicholson recorded the
different kinds of geometric shapes with which she and her fellow artists
in Paris were experimenting.

'Piet Mondrian was seeing the vertical against the horizontal. Ben
Nicholson was seeing the circle against the square: the rectangle is man's
calculation, the circle is a ball to hold in one's hand. I looked at the circle
in another way – as the vortex inside which the vital forces were generated
– and so, of course, to me the circle moved and became an ellipse. And so
it is that the ellipse was the central, the me, of my pictures; some motifs
generate within the ellipse, some travel out of it[9].' There is, perhaps, an
implication in this statement that the rectangle, or even other forms
bounded by a straight line, is a masculine form. In contrast then, the
ellipse or oval form, which can be symbolized by the egg, by a shape
pregnant with new life, stands as a feminine form. However, the question
of gender allied to forms cannot be pushed too far, because when Ben
Nicholson stayed in Paris in 1933 and was in contact with Winifred, he
produced an experimental painted panel which consisted of six circles
arranged within rectangular sections. She, on her part, painted a picture
P.134 entitled BLUE HEPTAGONS (circa 1936) in which the forms are bounded by
straight lines.

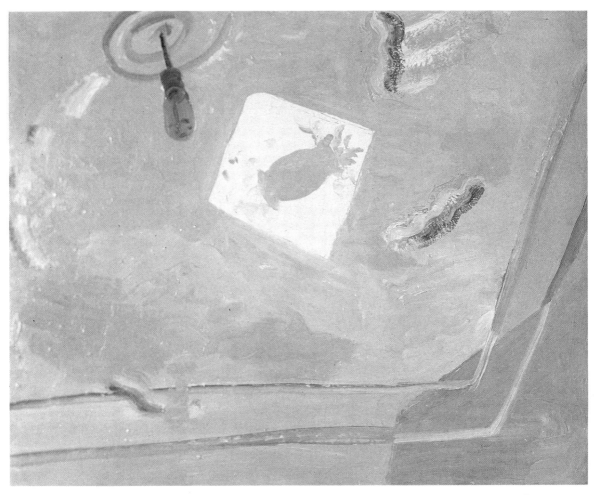

PARIS LIGHT
c.1933-4
—
OIL ON BOARD
59.7×75cm
PRIVATE COLLECTION

Her son Jake believes that Winifred Nicholson was intrigued by the shapes of some Montessori toys with which he played, and these toy shapes acted as the basis for the painting. Equally she was fascinated by artists' pigments (always buying the most expensive oil paints, Blockx, which she felt gave her the best texture and brilliance) and learnt of a new kind of blue, called Monastral Blue, newly developed by ICI and just available on the market. Possibly BLUE HEPTAGONS is the first picture to use the new blue pigment. A heptagon is a seven-sided shape, and of all numbers seven was the most significant for Winifred Nicholson. It stands for the days of the week, the seven notes of the musical scale and the seven colours of the spectral band of the rainbow. Since music and colour share a seven-fold division, Nicholson believed that this lent credence to her theory that colours were free and had the same independence as musical notes.

She produced many abstract paintings while in Paris – OUTWARD (1936) is an example where ellipses are used – but she never sent them for exhibition, either in Paris or in London, keeping them as a personal experiment that she would show fellow artists but not the public. Primarily she felt that ultimately she was a painter of objects found in the natural world, such as 'near, small, close things, like the faces of flowers and the glimmer of sunbeams that touch them.' Nicholson was able, during her Paris period, to paint both abstract and representational pictures, finding no conflict between the two. Since colour was her primary interest, it came first in the planning of a painting, and the subject matter followed on from this. She was equally at home making either a representational or an abstract painting as long as the work was true to her vision. She was able to move easily between the two modes of representation and abstraction since to her there was no clear division between them and this distinguishes her aesthetic; even her most representational works have an abstract, radiant quality. The two modes fed each other in a productive way; a letter from Winifred to Ben Nicholson reports that she is 'finding the constructive [her word for abstract] thing in the landscape.' As Christopher Neve wrote: 'After a time, she seems not so much to be painting as drifting hues into such relations to each other that they emit different qualities of light as you look at them. Perhaps that is one definition of painting.[10]'

Reputation and Innovation

When the Women's Purchase Committee of the Art Gallery of Ontario, Toronto, bought a painting by Winifred Nicholson entitled MRS CAMPBELL'S ROOM OF 1951, a view of wild flowers on a window-sill painted on the Isle of Canna, they sent her a questionnaire about the work. She duly filled it in and in the section called 'remarks on care and preservation' she wrote, with underlining 'Do not varnish – Do not keep in a dark cupboard'. These were heart-felt words; she hated the thought that when her paintings passed into the collections of public galleries, there would be times when, due to pressure of space, her work would be removed from view for a while and kept in a store-room. She wanted her paintings to be things that people lived with, and that ideally they should be seen in natural daylight, not always a possibility in some public galleries. A critic wrote of her work, when on exhibition in 1928, that 'her flower-pieces and landscapes make the most attractive wall-decorations which would enrich almost any room they hung in.' Although the main intention of this sentence was praise for her work, to call her work 'decoration' has a faintly pejorative air. It implies a sensitive arrangement of colours and shapes but all set down with a sense of vacancy, with nothing lying behind the colours and shapes. Nicholson, as we have seen, had particularly strong beliefs and ideas about the purpose and meaning of painting. Nevertheless there is no doubt that her paintings do 'enrich almost any room in which they are hung', and she would have endorsed this as a positive and valuable attribute.

Winifred Nicholson usually painted on a small scale, a domestic scale, since her average picture measures about 24 x 30 inches. Her friend, the poet Kathleen Raine, believes that, unlike Ben Nicholson who painted large works with a view to their hanging in public places, Winifred Nicholson painted for domestic settings. Two of her favourite exhibition spaces were Kettle's Yard Gallery in Cambridge, and the LYC Gallery in Brampton, Cumbria; the former run by Jim Ede and the latter by a Chinese artist Li Yuan Chia. Both these galleries were created from old houses and both were lived in by their creators, Jim Ede and Li Yuan Chia, close friends of hers. In fact, Ede, a friend from the 1920s, summed up Winifred Nicholson's work with the words 'companionable and universal'. By this he meant that her work had a particular and personal appeal for the viewer, as well as a place in a wider and more general context.

Winifred Nicholson exhibited recently executed work regularly at a handful of London commercial galleries from the 1920s to the 1970s. Her work sold quickly, usually going to a converted circle of private collectors. She liked to meet and talk with those people likely to buy her work, and from the 1960s on, she was a colourful feature in the gallery when her work was on show, often spending days on end sitting amid her pictures, talking to the public about art in general and her work in particular. Because her work sold to private collectors within a few days of the opening of any show, and because public institutions are much slower in their purchasing procedures, her work was not bought by large numbers of public galleries. The Contemporary Art Society, founded in 1910 specifically to purchase work by young British artists and donate it to public collections, is virtually the main channel by which Winifred Nicholson's work spread to the public galleries. Nicholson paintings in the public collections at Aberdeen, Newark, Nottingham and Cardiff found their way there by virtue of a donation from the Contemporary Art Society, and even her first representation at the Tate Gallery, WINDOW-SILL, LUGANO (1923), was a gift from the Contemporary Art Society in 1940, having originally been given to the society by the British collector and patron, Sir Edward Marsh, in 1927. Winifred Nicholson, unlike Ben Nicholson, did not put high prices on her paintings; however, London dealers would have had to sell her work at prices fixed in relation to the market for twentieth-century British pictures, and she would have had little control over this. However, her children remember how she would send pictures to local events such as Women's Institute charity sales in her native Cumbria, and would occasionally sell a work to an interested admirer who turned up at her farmhouse. This indicates the unworldly side of Winifred Nicholson; the side that prevented her from courting fame. Most other well-respected British artists of her ability and standing in the profession were much more protective about their work, and would have had strong ideas about the places where it should not be seen or exhibited. Nicholson did not appear to present a carefully constructed professional façade to the public eye. She did not, for example, keep the same kind of watchful and critical eye that Ben Nicholson kept over the presentation of his work in catalogues, books or exhibitions. She was happy to give paintings away to people who had borrowed them from her studio and enjoyed having them on their own walls; a sense of *enjoyment* of her work, of shared pleasure, was a priority.

Even though she came from a wealthy and titled family which gave her the time and space necessary to paint the paintings she wanted to make, there were times when she needed to sell pictures to raise some money, particularly when her three growing children were at school. A letter to Kathleen Raine written in 1949 shows something of her attitude to money: '...the power at the back of my pictures sold themselves to the exact amount I needed, i.e. Andrew's school fees for this last term which I had not paid, plus an overdraft at my bank...exactly the right amount'.[11]

Money was important when it was needed for pressing bills; beyond that Winifred was not a person who indulged herself in luxuries. She was teetotal all her life, and she made her own and her children's clothes, often improvising with unorthodox materials, once making a hat using foil milk-bottle tops as decoration.

Winifred Nicholson

Fabric Designs and Craft matters

From the time of her marriage in 1920, Winifred Nicholson's writings and paintings reveal an interest in patterned fabrics. When on her European travels, she collected peasant cloths and embroideries and at home, she liked to decorate her rooms with bold and colourful cloths and quilts. She was pleased to be asked to design a furnishing fabric, called 'constructive' in the publicity and titled SEQUENCE, for Alastair Morton's Edinburgh Weavers in 1937, along with other designers (including Ben Nicholson and Barbara Hepworth). A contemporary review described her design for curtain net as 'light and gay and free without the help of any colour – a delicate rhythm of changing shapes achieved by different weaves in the net. This is the kind of thing that those who must have net curtains are always looking for. It should have a great success....[12]' The success of Nicholson's design was helped by her inside knowledge of spinning and dyeing. She was always interested in traditional women's work within the craft traditions, and was delighted to discover that the farmer's wife, Mary Bewick, who lived next door to Bankshead, was a skilled rag rug maker. Rag – or hook rug making as it was called – was a cottage industry prevalent in Winifred Nicholson's part of Cumbria and she became a keen patron of this craft, providing materials, and supplying the inspiration for pattern design.

In the 1960s Winifred Nicholson liked to take painting holidays in Greece for not only did she find a warmer range of colours there and different varieties of wild flowers, but she liked to study and paint the Cretan and Minoan pottery figurines of Goddesses. Several of these appear in her paintings and it has since transpired that she had her own pet theory that these pottery figurines were made by Greek women artists. Believing this, she gave the Greek women potters, her artistic predecessors, her own form of painted homage.

Rainbows

The last five years of Winifred Nicholson's long life were spent, typically, in new colour adventures. At the age of eighty-two she purchased two small glass prisms, which she called her portable rainbow machines, and she looked through these to find subjects to paint. When you hold a prism close to your eye and look through it at a vase of flowers on a window-sill, an object set against the light, the outer edges of the object have a halo of rainbow colours, because the light rays are broken down into their seven spectral bands. Such a discovery delighted Winifred Nicholson who painted several pictures in celebration of this.

P.153   ACCORD, (1978), painted when she was eighty-four, is one of these

NIGHT AND DAY
c.mid 1970's

———

HOOKED RUG – MADE
BY MARY BERWICK
FROM A DESIGN BY
WINIFRED NICHOLSON.
125×87cm
ARTIST'S FAMILY
REPRODUCED BY
ARRANGEMENT WITH
SHIPLEY ART GALLERY

THE GATE TO THE ISLES
1980
—
OIL ON CANVAS
45.7×61cm
PRIVATE COLLECTION

rainbow pictures. It depicts two rounded glass vessels on a window-sill with foliage seen beyond. The composition is based upon semi-circular forms, which break like waves upon the scene, taking their centre of energy from the half-seen sun-like form at the bottom of the picture. The two glass vessels float in the midst of this pulsating colour and provide suitable companions for each other; COMPANIONS is in fact the alternative title for this work. PRISMATIC FIRE is another extraordinary late work, a 'flowers on a window-sill' picture taken to the edge of abstraction, the vivid, saturated colours seeming to catch alight in front of our eyes. It has the intensity of the last dying rays of a sunset as they catch the rim of an object, but is also flooded with the ephemeral beauty of a rainbow.

P.154

In a series of letters written to a research physicist in the last few months of her life, Winifred Nicholson discussed with him her favourite life-long themes of light and colour. For her these two things were the most important things in the universe, and in one letter she equated the liberating quality of colour with that of love: 'And so all paradoxes can be surmounted by Love or shall we say colour. Is that why my heart leaps up when I behold a rainbow in the sky?'

Winifred Nicholson was a complex person, but she had an *uncomplicated* attitude to life. She had faith, optimism, and enthusiasm and she remained open to new and experimental ideas until the end of her life. Endings, however, were not to be taken too literally – they could be the beginning of a form of life, a new kind of perception. Nicholson's impressive and vibrant body of work opens our eyes to the furthest horizons of colour and light.

Winifred Nicholson

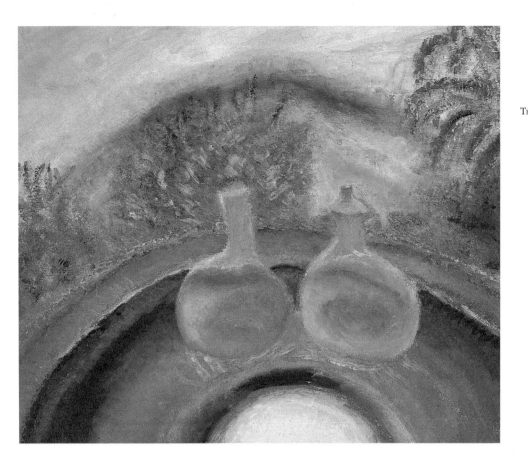

ACCORD
1978
—
OIL ON CANVAS
63.5×77.5cm
THE ARTIST'S FAMILY

Winifred Nicholson

PRISMATIC FIVE

1979

———

OIL ON CANVAS

61×61cm

THE ARTIST'S FAMILY

Eileen Agar

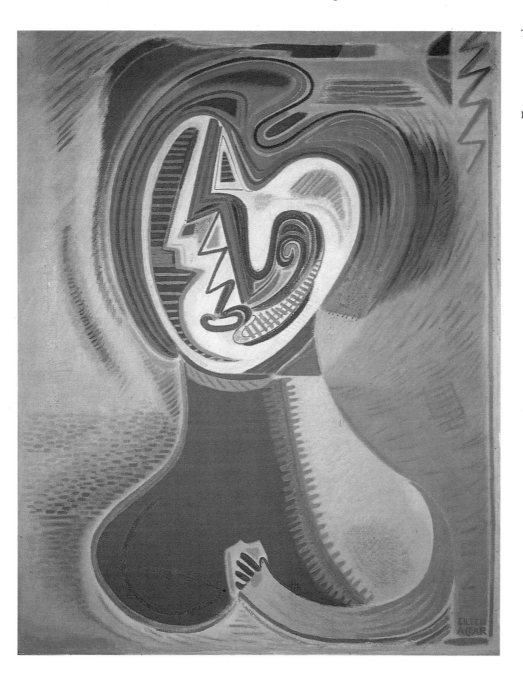

The Modern Muse
1931

—

Oil on canvas
101.6×81.28cm
Private collection

Eileen Agar

Eileen Agar with
Ceremonial Hat for
eating Bouillabaisse

———

Artist's collection
Photo Adrian Arbib

Angel of Anarchy
(second version)
1940-3

———

Plaster cast
covered with
mixed media
70×30.5×30.5cm
Tate Gallery
London

Eileen Agar

Oval Object
1953
—
Pastel
31.11 × 22.22cm
Private collection

THE SLEEPWALKERS

1979

—

ACRYLIC ON CANVAS

101.6×127cm

BIRCH & CONRAN

EILEEN AGAR
b . 1 8 9 9

'Art or Life: it is never either/or, it is always both.'

Within the limited terms of traditional art history, Eileen Agar appears
briefly centre stage. Her relationship with Surrealism, for all its
ambivalence, has assured her a place in histories of modernism denied the
other artists in this book. Yet, as with Carrington, Knight, Hamnett and
Nicholson, her role as a woman artist in an essentially masculine domain
has structured and directed the production and consumption of her art.
While her work is possibly more cosmopolitan and urbane than that of,
say, Hamnett or Knight, it unites the aesthetics of Carrington and
Nicholson, with its subtle blend of the decorative and the abstract. Her
'objects', collages and paintings implicitly raise issues of gender and
representation, exploring the nature of female creativity[1].

The position of the woman artist within Surrealism is also complex
and highlights many of the wider issues of woman's relationship to art
practice and theory within a society structured by essentially masculine
values – the work of women such as Agar being both central to the
concerns of Surrealism and marginalized by it; seen to illustrate its aims
yet be produced outside of its parameters. The inclusion of the work of
women artists in the main surrealist exhibitions helped to demonstrate
that movements break from established ideas of high art. However, none
of the main female contributors to surrealist shows were recognized as
core members of the group. Agar's art has long outlived the formal
existence of the Surrealist movement but the philosophies of poets such as
André Breton and Paul Eluard hover ghost-like over her critical
reputation. Luckily, she has survived to see a greater recognition of her
personal aesthetic and of her contribution to British art[2].

Finding a Voice

Eileen Agar was born into a wealthy Anglo-Argentine family in Buenos
Aires in 1899 and spent her early life in a 'soft web of lilac, flowers and
good air[3]'. Cushioned from economic hardship she grew up in a world of
cultured luxury which endowed her with an elegant assurance and the
ability to reject the stifling morality and conventional expectations of her
family. Her early interest in art was tolerated, even encouraged, as an
acceptable feminine pastime. In 1920 Mamie Agar even employed a
teacher of watercolour for her daughter. For Agar herself, however, the
commitment to a career as an artist was compelling, leading her first to
classes in the studio of the sculptor Leon Underwood[4] and then, in 1921

to the Slade. Even in the 1920s art teaching at the Slade remained removed from the avant-garde experimentation of the European Modernists, and stressed a representational art, strongly dependent on figure study and the traditions of landscape.

Carrington's teacher, Tonks, whose antagonism to the new European art has become legendary, still determined much of the Slade's teaching practice. Agar was set to work copying classical busts and drawing from male and female models. Her progress was respectable but unremarkable. The experience of formal teaching consolidated her intentions to become a painter but did little to awaken a more personal style. The most important aspect of her time at the Slade appears to have been the company of other artists. At Underwood's she had studied with Henry Moore, Gertrude Hermes and the architect Rodney Thomas, who introduced Agar to the modernist aesthetic of Le Corbusier. To this circle was added a young painter, Robin Bartlett, who was to become Agar's first husband and means of escape from the control of her family. In 1924, with Bartlett, Agar travelled to Paris and then Spain discovering the imaginative power of Goya and El Greco, a welcome antidote to the Slade's gentlemanly restraint.

The exhilaration of new-found freedom began to give way to the realisation that married life also carried unacceptable constraints. Agar still found it difficult to define her own artistic style, despite her increasing involvement in the self-consciously bohemian London art world. The need to assert an independent identity remained a major issue in her life. She had exchanged the role of daughter for that of wife but found both lacking. The most dramatic change of direction occurred in 1926 with the beginning of what was to be a life-long relationship with a charismatic Hungarian writer Joseph Bard. Seven years older than Agar, Bard's intellectual assurance and sophistication served to consolidate her own artistic confidence. A work from this period SELF-PORTRAIT 1927 signalled a new direction for Agar, she had as she saw it 'thrown off the shackles and started a new life[5]'. Although a strong work, there is little of the artist's later formal wit and adventurousness in this image. It does, however, reveal a highly skilled and accomplished artist, a confident recognition of a confident self.

Abstract Beginnings

In 1929, on the advice of the Russian artist Boris Anrep, Agar and Bard moved to Paris. Here Agar hoped to escape the insularity so valued by institutions such as the Slade. Setting up a studio in the Rue Schoelcher, she became a frequent visitor to the Jardin des Plantes. The collection there enthralled Agar, in particular the fossils with 'their muted colour

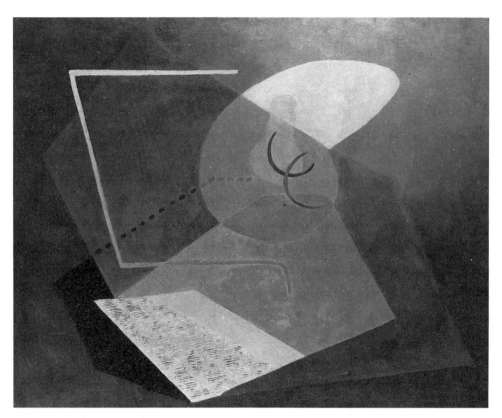

MOVEMENT IN SPACE
1931
———
OIL ON CANVAS
76.2×91.44cm
PRIVATE COLLECTION

SELF-PORTRAIT
1927
———
OIL ON CANVAS
76.2×64.13cm
NATIONAL PORTRAIT
GALLERY, LONDON

PORTRAIT OF
JOSEPH BARD
———
PEN AND INK
PRIVATE COLLECTION

and embedded beauty[6]'. The enigmatic subtlety of such examples of nature's transformational powers became the basis of a new aesthetic for Agar. Adding to her own growing interest in natural formations was the influence of the abstract Cubist painter Foltyn. From this Czech artist Agar learned the formalist games of the Cubists, with their denial of illusionistic space and perspective, and gained a greater sensitivity to the abstract values of colour, space and composition. These new priorities were consolidated by contact with the sculptor Brancusi, to whom Agar was introduced by Ezra Pound. The purity of line intrinsic to Brancusi's sculptural forms plus his interest in embryonic shapes seems to underlie a work such as Agar's MOVEMENT IN SPACE of 1931. The timeless, archaic quality injected into much of Agar's work also reflects shared interests with Brancusi and his passion for early sculptural forms.

As a woman artist the search for essential forms had a particular resonance for Agar. In the December 1931 edition of *The Island* (a literary journal founded by Bard and Agar) Agar contributed a short piece on what she called 'womb-magic, the dominance of female creativity and imagination', where she makes conscious links between physical and artistic conception.

These ideas surface most dramatically in her 1933-34 work
P.156   AUTOBIOGRAPHY OF AN EMBRYO. This large painting is in sharp contrast to the unassuming self-portrait of six years earlier. It weaves together classical allegory with abstract forms, introducing enduring elements of Agar's symbolic repertoire such as the outstretched palm, shell and plant structures, and the almost scientific interest in embryology. These motifs are introduced like bizarre heraldic images, linked together by the painting's underlying black structure which unites the canvas's bright primary colours.

At first it appears like a huge Technicolor enlargement of a microscopic slide and then the amoeba-like shapes form themselves into more directly symbolic images. Imagery of the womb, the egg and the foetus give a physical and ritualized form to the process of creativity and act as a metaphor for culture itself. In Agar's symbolic language physical procreation is seen as analogous to artistic invention, to represent the most simple yet complete reference to human cultural endeavours. (Ironically, Agar made a conscious decision not to have children herself as she felt motherhood would hamper her work.) The play between figuration and abstraction, between decorative patterning and organic form, apparent in this work, remain the essential characteristics of Agar's aesthetic throughout her career.

In Paris Agar had met André Breton and Paul Eluard, the leading figures of Surrealism (at that time the dominant art movement among French avant-garde writers and artists), but remained removed from the movement proper. As part of the same social grouping, she undoubtedly imbibed some of its formulae and creative devices, yet the dogma of Surrealism, its fascination with the dream and the unconscious, did not consciously affect Agar until later in the 1930s. In this sense Agar was not alone. Surrealism had little direct impact in Britain before its dramatic arrival in 1936 with the opening of the International Surrealist Exhibition[7] at the New Burlington Galleries in London. Many British artists were aware of surrealist work in France but tended to view it through a more generalized modernist interest in Picasso.

A work such as Agar's THE MODERN MUSE of 1931 is an interesting example of this rather freeflowing transference of ideas. The similarity of this image to the work of Picasso during the same period is undeniable, but if anything Agar's painting prefigures Picasso's obssesive drawings and sculptures of a woman's head of 1932-33[8]. In these works he makes great play on the transmutability of his images, constructing his model's head out of a series of highly phallic shapes, conflating desire with its object.

P.155 Agar's neck and head in THE MODERN MUSE suggests more of a synthesis of both male and female biomorphic forms, the artist's muse is no longer a passive, objectified female but a symbol of active sexuality. The combined male and female characteristics present a pictographic image of both sexual and artistic creativity.

The ability of the unconscious mind to superimpose the fantastic and the imagined on to external objects, was an essential tool of the surrealists. Yet it emerges as a device of Agar's on a determinedly conscious level. Surface similarities exist between the work of Agar and her more famous contemporaries, symptomatic of their shared interests in the archaic past and the primitive. However, active involvement in the theoretical debates of Breton and his followers only emerged in Agar's work after the 1936 exhibition.

Agar spent the summer of 1935 in Swanage and had met and become friendly with the painter Paul Nash, who at that time was one of the few British artists to be immersed in surrealist ideas about representation. The ensuing exchange of ideas between Agar and Nash was to be highly productive for both artists. Nash's interest in photography and the symbolic function of landscape struck a chord with Agar's increasing awareness of the transformational powers of nature. Agar became fascinated by the flotsam and jetsam of the Dorset beaches, collecting bizarre objects such as the fragment of shell-encrusted anchor chain later included in Nash's photomontage of SWANAGE. Objects such as this combined the qualities of the Jardin des Plantes fossils, what Agar called 'signals in time, isolated objects which take on the importance of a problem resolved at some moment far back in the mists of memory'[9] with the mysterious presence of an equally forgotten human intervention.

The SEASHORE MONSTER, as Nash called this found object, represents a meeting point of surrealist thought and Agar's more personal search for what she saw as an essentially female contribution to modernist aesthetics. Created by man, nature and chance in equal combination, the encrusted anchor chain provided an ideal metaphor for creativity itself. In its original state it had represented the coupling of the man-made and the natural, but it was 'metamorphosed by the sea into a new creation, a bird snake'[10]. This transformation of the mundane into the impossible was an essential characteristic of Surrealism, a concrete reference to Lautréamont's revered lines '...as beautiful as the chance encounter on a dissecting table of a sewing machine and an umbrella...'[11]. Like the objects refered to within the surrealist credo, Agar's bird snake also functions as a sexual metaphor, its transformation occurring through the interpenetration of opposites. As Agar puts it 'The sea and the land sometimes play together like man and wife, and achieve astonishing results.'[12]

The attributed meanings of such found objects are explicitly gendered within the traditions of Graeco-Roman culture. Basic matter, the earth, is seen as both passive and feminine; whereas the action of transforming the earth, is active and masculine. In the metamorphosed object, as was also the case in Agar's MODERN MUSE, is a manifestation of the unification of these dualities. It is the search for this moment of equilibrium, the harmonious inter-dependence of masculine and female principles of creativity where gender differences are recognized yet given equal status, that underpins Agar's art.

Agar and Surrealism

The summer in Swanage injected a new coherence into Agar's style and also led indirectly to her first real contact with mainstream Surrealism. Through Nash, Agar was recommended to the two British organizers of the 1936 exhibition, Herbert Read and Roland Penrose. In the spring of 1936 they visited Agar's studio and, impressed with her work, Read and Penrose chose three oil paintings and five objects. Although previously unaware of the formal pre-requisites of the surrealist movement Agar willingly (if rather sceptically) became one of the small English contingent of the show. As she was later to put it 'One day I was an artist exploring highly personal combinations of form and content, and the next I was calmly informed I was a Surrealist!'[13]

The assimilation of disparate artists into the core grouping of surrealist poets and painters was a frequently used tactic, in keeping with the wider aims of the movement. Surrealism was determined to unleash the subjugated power of the human unconscious, to assert a superior reality in 'the omnipotence of the dream, and in the disinterested play of thought'[14]. For the surrealist artist, however, the visual realization of such aims remained problematic. The recognition of surrealist qualities within existing material was a far simpler procedure. Surrealist magazines and literature were often devoted to the work of 'chosen artists', individuals who, like Agar, had produced material conforming to surrealist thinking yet were outside of its sphere of influence. Artefacts from previously marginalized groups, whether the insane, the naïve or the non-European, were embraced by Breton and his followers as exemplifying an art produced outside of conventional European aesthetics or moral concerns.

Possibly the most important of the works by Agar in the 1936 exhibition was QUADRIGA. The painting is an interesting mix of both order and the surrealist technique of automatism, where by drugs, hypnosis or various other trance states the artist attempts to subvert rational control of her composition. There is an immediate similarity to the work of the surrealist painter André Masson, who was also showing at the London exhibition and according to Agar '…set a universe in motion with his menacing insect ballet in green, yellow and blue'[15]. Comparison of the two artists is in fact revealing of some important divergences.

Agar's painting is made up of the same play on patterning and freeflowing line as her earlier AUTOBIOGRAPHY OF AN EMBRYO. Each of its four sharply divided sections are filled with the same design of a horse's head, yet the heads are all unique in themselves. As in earlier works her inspiration is sculptural. The horse's heads come not from nature but from an ancient Greek frieze[16]. Over the surface of these forms Agar has allowed her brush to roam in almost chaotic freedom, producing a sharp contrast between random shapes and the classical heads. While the initial appearance of the work evokes the automatist principles of an artist such as Masson, the chance elements of the painting are subsumed by the ordered composition.

Masson, when asked about his approach to art, was insistent on the pre-eminent importance of the moment of metamorphosis, the point at which a line is about to attain recognisable meaning. Agar's work imposes order first and then plays with disintegrating that meaning. P.157 QUADRIGA is in fact a very rational work, carefully constructed and charged with literary meaning. According to Agar the painting incorporated themes from classical art and literature with her own childhood memories yet the final outcome is archetypal rather than fantastic.

The 1936 New Burlington Gallery exhibition of Surrealism attracted considerable public attention, the work of the more established

THE SEASHORE
MONSTER
1935
—
OBJECT (DESTROYED)
PHOTO COURTESY OF
THE ARTIST

GROUP PHOTOGRAPH
OF PARTICIPANTS OF THE
INTERNATIONAL
SURREALIST
EXHIBITION
1936
AT THE BURLINGTON
GALLERIES, LONDON
———
(BACK ROW, L TO R)
RUPERT LEE, ... SALVADOR

DALI, PAUL ELUARD,
ROLAND PENROSE,
HERBERT READ,
E.L.T. MESENS,
GEORGE REAVEY,
HUGH SYRES-DAVIES
(FRONT ROW, L TO R)
DIAN BRINTON LEE,
NUSCH ELUARD,
EILEEN AGAR,
SHEILA LEGGE

Europeans conferring a reflected notoriety on a young generation of British artists. Agar's search for a language of female creativity intersected with the Surrealist fascination with social difference and deviancy, what was constructed as 'otherness' to a dominant white, masculine, and middle-class culture. Predominantly male as the Surrealist movement undoubtedly was, it saw the work of women artists such as Agar, Meret Oppenheim, Frida Kahlo or Ithell Colqhoun as representative of new, intrinsically surreal, pictorial values. Although many women, like Agar, exhibited in Surrealist exhibitions or contributed to its journals, few saw themselves as actually part of the movement itself[17], and their assimilation remained tokenistic rather than actual.

Membership to that club appears to have been determinedly masculine. Despite, or perhaps because of this intrinsic masculinity, the surrealist aesthetic is based on a recognition of the fundamentally gendered nature of traditional forms of representation. As a movement it may not question the nature of patriarchy but it at least recognizes its existence. The fact that desire and sexuality play a pre-eminent role in much surrealist work, forces an understanding of the presupposed gender of both artist and audience, a recognition frequently subsumed in less overtly masculine art.

In this sense the work of women associated with the Surrealists is often unusually assertive of its function as 'Woman's Art'. Traditional denials of female rationality, of the ability of women to think on an abstract level, combined with equally long-standing associations with nature and the natural, freed their art from the civilized values so detested by the surrealists.

The art of women, like much non-European art, was seen by Surrealists like Breton as exemplifying both otherness and the repressed, and as such presented a concrete realization of the human unconscious. Many of the surrealist challenges to bourgeois morality are explicitly sexual, confronting the traditions of voyeurism and eroticism in European art. Yet while self-conscious of such issues, the sexual status of women within Surrealism is still secondary. The arguments are laid out but the authoritative voice is still that of the male artist or poet.

P.158 Agar's most famous work is probably her ANGEL OF ANARCHY the first version of which was exhibited at the 1938 International Surrealist exhibition in Amsterdam. The second version of the work, now in the Tate Gallery, was produced in 1940 and is an almost perfect encapsulation of the Surrealist aesthetic while remaining a very female work. Its swathes of silk and beads give the dislocated head a magical, ritual appearance, purposeful and mysterious at the same time. Formally the work is a rejection of the materials of fine art. The plaster cast of a male head, recognizable as having been produced within the conventions of

Eileen Agar

ANGEL OF ANARCHY
(FIRST VERSION)
1937
—
LOST
PHOTO COURTESY OF
THE ARTIST

traditional sculpture was initially painted and decorated to resemble a bizarre tribal object, more Maori head than portrait bust.

After the first version went missing, Agar elaborated on the initial work, completely obscuring the plaster beneath fragments of embroidered cloth. The result is both luxuriant and vaguely threatening, an elegant monster. This combination of attractiveness with enigmatic danger epitomizes the Surrealists' approach to female sexuality; an exquisitely obscure object of desire. The skills used to construct the work are those traditionally perceived as feminine. The object is dressed and decorated, the materials are also very obviously female, fragments of an affluent and glamorous wardrobe. What you are finally confronted with is the all encompassing power of such materials and skills to transform the mundane into the exotic.

As with QUADRIGA, the element of allegory remains, the title of the work ANGEL OF ANARCHY imparting it with a series of associated meanings. Does it refer to the Spanish civil war? Is it a reference to the character of Herbert Read or the countenance of Joseph Bard?[18]. In the end the mystery of the work is its essence, it prompts no desire to unwrap the piece, to see what lies within. The external disguise is far more alluring than whatever it might hide. It seems particularly like Agar to re-assert the importance of the decorative while also imparting the work with a colder level of threat. In ANGEL OF ANARCHY, Agar is also searching for the same sexual synthesis of earlier works; the male head produced with the materials of a masculine language of art united with the explicitly female skills and materials. In this later work, however, there is no doubt as to which sex has the upper hand.

Agar's entrance into the more glamorous world of the international avant-garde was consolidated by a trip to Mougins in the South of France in the summer of 1937. The invitation to spend the summer in France emerged through an increasingly intimate friendship with Paul and Nusch Eluard. Agar and Bard joined Roland Penrose and the photographer Lee Miller, to become part of a group dominated by the charismatic personality of Picasso. Agar was delighted to find their shared interests leading to praise from the increasingly lionized artist. The interest of Picasso in the found object and collage techniques was a vindication of Agar's own aesthetic, and she continued to use bits of weathered cork and wood, shells and stones to produce mysterious objects such as MARINE OBJECT (1939). The beach both as a source of material and a phenomenon, continued to exert a powerful fascination. The meeting of sea and land remained an important motif emerging even in a work such as BATTLE CRY/BULLET PROOF PAINTING (1938), with its ostensible reference to the approaching disaster of the Second World War.

Like QUADRIGA, BATTLE CRY harnesses chance effects, here the spilling of molten lead, to produce a work both enigmatic yet accessible. This work was at first an attempt to employ totally automatist techniques, yet as Agar describes, the end product was fairly controlled '...the end result was a mixture I found satisfying, but which could hardly qualify as pure automatism. For me intuition combined with controlled emotion and intellectual consideration produce the best effects.'[19] The separate elements of the painting merge organically into each other as the lead sprawls across the surface of the picture plane (which is in fact metal rather than canvas) resembling some strange form of seaweed thrown up on a sandy beach. Again Agar has produced a hybrid creature, half-plant, half-crustacean, both frightening and attractive. In its physical composition BATTLE CRY continues to utilize non-fine art materials; the metal, lead and plaster counter-balancing the almost whimsical attractiveness of what is essentially a serious work.

P.158   The element of whimsy is more apparent in Agar's obviously humorous CEREMONIAL HAT FOR EATING BOUILLABAISSE (1936)[20], a parody of the ritual function of human dress, which despite its humour shares the essential characteristics of Agar's art. It is to all intents and purposes an 'object' such as the Seashore Monster, yet by being worn it is removed from the realm of contemplation to that of decoration.

Womb Magic

The destructive horror of the Second World War cut into Agar's career, her harmonious and elegant style finding little outlet in the dark world of the London Blitz. On a personal level the war years saw the consolidation of her relationship to Bard, whom she married in 1940, and a reconciliation with her now ailing and alcoholic mother. The affluence of her childhood had become a distant memory of another world and her career as an artist was now the dominant reality of her life.

Agar's pre-war involvement with Surrealism was to have a double-edged effect on her professional reputation. On one hand she had received great public attention by being seen as the main British woman Surrealist. However her work also remained categorized as reflective of the ideas of the group as a whole, a categorization that denied many of the more interesting aspects of Agar's work. Her paintings and collages of the post-war period continued to explore the nature and gender of the languages of art in a coherent and fluent manner. Yet they lacked the element of surrealist outrageousness, never really part of Agar's style, but increasingly expected by a public used to the antics of artists such as Dali.

The comparison with Dali is particularly interesting in the context of works such as the recent series of paintings based on photographs taken by Agar of rocks at Ploumanach in Brittany. Many of Dali's works

MARINE OBJECT
1939
—
ARTIST'S COLLECTION

BATTLE CRY/BULLET
PROOF PAINTING
1938
—
LEAD, PAINT AND
PLASTER ON METAL
53.2×81.1cm
COLLECTION OF
GORDON ONSLOW
FORD

EILEEN WEARING
CEREMONIAL HAT FOR
EATING BOUILLABAISSE
c.1936
—

The Rocks at
Ploumanach,
Brittany
c.1985
—
Private collection

derive from forms suggested by the rock formations of the beaches of his
home at Port Lligat, the complex conjunction of his memories and desires
imposing themselves on the natural world. In this process, which Dali
called his 'paranoic-critical method' the outside world acts as a mirror of
the artist's unconscious. Agar's fascination with the suggestive forms of
the Ploumanach rocks, however, reveals not her personal fantasies but her
recognition of the magical and comic power of nature itself.

In the post-war period Agar's work slipped into a less public if
equally prolific phase; fuelled by frequent winter visits to what was then
the unspoilt beauty of Tenerife[21]. The fact that the work of this period has
received relatively little critical attention is in itself interesting, especially
since the formal devices of Agar's aesthetic share characteristics with
Abstract Expressionism, or the 'New York School', the dominant art
movement of the post-war period which was itself based on theories of
automatism and universal symbolism[22].

This relative lack of recognition is in direct contrast to the position
of a surrealist artist such as Masson, whose stylistic affinities with Agar
have already been mentioned. His paintings are often given greater
significance by their perceived links to the style of the New York school;
the gift of historical hindsight conferring on his art a directional quality
outside of the intrinsic interest of the work itself. It seems strange that
just at the moment when vital components of Agar's personal style were
gaining enormous international acceptance, her own work was receiving
less attention.

P.159 The element of surrealist technique of most appeal to a younger
generation of artists in the 1950s was undoubtedly automatism. Yet as
with Agar, the formal mechanics of automatic painting were combined
with a fascination with archetypal imagery – the belief in a universal
symbolic language. Again, as Agar had done in the 1930s, Abstract
Expressionists such as Jackson Pollock sought to unite the free flow of
the artist's hand with the production of 'essential' forms. While not
denying the many differences between these artists and Agar, there are
equally many ways in which Agar's work of the 1950s is wonderfully
apposite of that period.

Why this fact, and her own formal prescience, have gone largely
unobserved is puzzling. A possible explanation may lie in the almost
obsessive masculinity attributed to both the movement and its main
protagonists[23]. The frequently mythologized figure of Pollock, is the art
critics' cross between James Dean and Marlon Brando, exuding on canvas
the same rebellious, macho sexuality as such screen idols. Similarly,
discussion of the work of Abstract Expressionists abounds with highly

gender-laden adjectives, it is 'strong' 'incisive', 'thrusting' and 'aggressive'. Its image of barely controlled violence is reinforced by the frequent title of 'Action Painting', all these elements conforming to popular perceptions of masculinity.

Agar's 'womb magic' was not reconcilable with the assertive maleness of the dominant art trends. Cultural stereotypes of female passivity made the function of the female artist within 'Action Painting' difficult to define, hence the often peripheral position allocated to artists such as Lee Krasner or Helen Frankenthaler[24]. Its pre-eminence as a movement also affected the careers of artists such as Agar; in art as in so many other areas of activity, women were denied a central role in post-war western culture.

P.160   The recognition of women artists prompted by the growth of the feminist movement in the 1960s and 1970s, has led to a greater awareness of the problems that such artists have had to confront in constructing a coherent style. Agar, who has continued to work energetically, has been able to see a revival of interest in her art and a more sympathetic appraisal of the post-war work. Eileen Agar's belief in the power of female imagery, her interest in sexual archetypes and subversion of traditional materials of fine art all serve to deny the inviolability of the male artist. Her work may not be self-conciously feminist but it is certainly an assertion of women's art.

NOTES

INTRODUCTION

1. Fry, Roger, Preface to exhibition catalogue *The New Movement in Art,* Birmingham, July-Sept., 1917

2. Fry, Roger 'An Essay in Aesthetics,' *Vision & Design,* 1961, p.32.

CHAPTER ONE

1. Knight, Laura *Magic of a Line* William Kimber, London, 1965, p.26

2. Knight, Laura *Oil Paint and Grease Paint* (all quotations are from the Penguin edition, 1941) p.12

3. Knight, *ibid.* 1941, p.7

4. Knight, *ibid.* 1965, p.24

5. Knight, *ibid.* 1941, p.59

6. Knight, *ibid.* 1941, p.77

7. Bastien-Lepage was a late nineteeth-century French painter who made realism in the depiction of rural peasant's lives the most important aspect of his work.

8. Knight, *ibid.* 1965, p.117

9. Knight, *ibid.* 1965, p.135

10. See the Newlyn catalogues by Caroline Fox (details in select bibliography), and *British Impressionism: A Garden of Bright Images* by Laura Wortley.

11. Knight, *ibid.* 1941, p.172

12. Knight, *ibid.* 1941, p.175

13. Knight, *ibid.* 1941, p.188

14. Knight, *ibid.* 1941, p.233

15. Knight, *ibid.* 1941, p.243

16. Quoted by David Phillips in the appendix to *Laura Knight* by Janet Dunbar.

17. Daily Mail October 23rd 1930.

18. Knight, *ibid.* 1965, p.203

19. Knight, *ibid.* 1965, p.203

20. Knight, *ibid.* 1965, p.224

21. See *British Impressionism* by Kenneth McConkey, Phaidon 1989.

22. Knight, *ibid.* 1965, p.307

23. Letter dated 10th December 1940 to the War Artists Advisory Committee, in the Imperial War Museum archive.

24. Quoted in newspaper article about Laura Knight by Margaret Laing.

25. Knight, Laura, 4th May 1922.

26. *War Pictures by British Artists* with an Introduction by Laura Knight.

CHAPTER TWO

1. Hamnett, Nina *Laughing Torso* Constable, London, 1932, republished by Virago Press, London 1984, p.16 (all quotes are taken from the Virago edition)

2. Hamnett, *ibid.,* p.42

3. *Birmingham Evening Dispatch,* 6th July 1928

4. Hamnett, *ibid.,* p.39

5. Life and Letters 'The Late W. H. Davies', 9th July 1942

6. Hamnett, *ibid.,* p.49

7. Hamnett, *ibid.,* p52

8. Hamnett, *ibid.,* p.219

9. George Cruikshank (1792-1878), English actor and political cartoonist; Honoré Daumier (1810-79), French painter and political caricaturist; Thomas Rowlandson (1756-1827) also a caricaturist, providing humorous comments on the London social scene.

10. *Art Work,* Vol.1 no.2, October 1924 p.112

11. Hamnett, *ibid.,* p.110

12. Review of Nina Hamnett's work in *The Times,* 15 May 1926

13. Hamnett, *ibid.*, p.37

14. *The Outlook*, 1927

15. Hamnett, *ibid.*, p.9

16. See *Nina Hamnett: Queen of Bohemia* by Denise Hooker, Chapters 14 & 15, 'Fitzrovia' and 'Candlelight', and *'Soho in the Fifties'* by Daniel Farson.

CHAPTER THREE

1. Michael Holroyd's exhaustive biography of Lytton Strachey (first published 1967-68) was among the most influential of such books, as well as Quentin Bell's biography of Virginia Woolf (1972). The list of books on the Bloomsbury Group would need a whole bibliography to itself. For a personal account of life with Carrington and Lytton Strachey, see *Memories* by Francis Partridge.

2. 'Carrington. *Letters and Extracts From Her Diaries*', edited by David Garnett. Oxford University Press 1979.

3. Rosamond Lehmann in conversation with the author.

4. See Exhibition Catalogue for *British Art in the Twentieth Century*, at the Royal Academy 1986.

5. From *Selected Letters of Mark Gertler*, Ed. Noel Carrington, Hart Davis 1965.

6. See 'The Fresco Revival in the Early Twentieth Century' by Alan Powers, in *The Journal of the Decorative Arts Society*, no.12 1988.

7. Among known works lost are: nursery doors painted for Rosamond Lehmann, a panel for Henry Lamb's house, painted decoration for Julia Strachey, pub signs, cellar door and bathroom tiles at Ham Spray, many fireplace tiles, decorations for Alix and James Strachey's rooms in London, as well as for Lytton's London flat, and several painted trunks.

8. Fry's theories are laid out most clearly in his collected essays, *Vision and Design*, first published 1920.

9. For a sustained critique of Fry's position, see *English Post-Impressionism* by Simon Watney, who suggests that Fry was blinded by his enthusiasm for French art to local traditions in English art and its strengths.

10. The success of books like Jocasta Innes's *Paintability*, a plethora of magazine articles on do-it-yourself interior design with an emphasis on hand-painted surfaces, a renewal of public commissions to decorative artists and the commercial availability of decorated pottery and chinaware – all indicate a re-awakening of interest in the decorative arts on a scale which would have been impossible at the time Omega existed.

11. Letter to Gerald Brenan, December 18 1921.

12. Letter to Margaret Waley c. 1930, The Tate Gallery Archive.

13. See *Loved Ones Pen Portraits* by Diana Mosley, Sidgwick & Jackson, 1985, chapter entitled 'Lytton Strachey and Carrington'.

14. Letter to Alix Strachey, February 4th 1924 or 1925. British Museum Manuscripts Department.

15. From Partridge, *ibid.*

16. Carrington met Ralph Partridge in 1918 through her brother Noel. Partridge later fell in love with Carrington and insisted that they marry. By that time he had become part of the household at Tidmarsh and Carrington was afraid that refusing him would undermine the stability of her relationship with Lytton Strachey, who was himself attracted to Partridge. They married but their relationship was quickly undermined by the fact that Carrington had started having an affair with Partridge's best friend Gerald Brenan. Ralph Partridge continued living with Carrington and Strachey until their deaths and was an important person in both their lives. For a first hand account of this complicated scenario see Frances Partridge, *ibid.*

17. *Drawn From Life* by Stella Bowen, reprinted by Virago Press Ltd. 1984. Stella Bowen was married to the writer Ford Madox Ford and understood the dilemmas of nurturing another person's career at the expense of one's own.

18. Undated letter c. 1921 British Museum Manuscripts Department.

19. From Carrington's Diary undated, British Museum Manuscripts Department.

20. Letter dated March 15th, probably 1922 or 1923, British Museum Manuscripts Department.

21. Letter to Alix Strachey, undated, British Museum Manuscripts Department.

22. See *Julia: A Portrait of Julia Strachey By Herself and Frances Partridge*, Penguin Books 1984, which includes *Carrington: A Study of a Modern Witch*.

CHAPTER FOUR

1. 'Blinks', *Unknown Colour* p.24

2. 'The Points of View of Winifred Nicholson' by Christopher Neve, *Unknown Colour*, p.20

3. Undated letter to Jake Nicholson, *Unknown Colour*, p.233

4. 'Moments of Light', *Unknown Colour*, p.37

5. Letter to Ben Nicholson, 1932, quoted in *Unknown Colour*, p.139

6. 'Blinks', *Unknown Colour*, p.24

7. 'Paris in the 1920s and 1930s', *Unknown Colour*, p.105

8. 'Paris in the 1920s and 1930s', *Unknown Colour*, p.106

9. 'Three Kinds of Artists', *Unknown Colour*, p.239

10. Neve, *ibid.*, *Unknown Colour*, p.20

11. *Unknown Colour* p.205

12. Anon review, 'Pins and Needles', *Night and Day*, Vol.1, no.20, p.20

CHAPTER FIVE

1. In her autobiography Agar recounts a conversation with the artist and designer, Marcel Breuer: '...he thought that women are or should be the real Surrealists because of the metamorphic changes in the womb when they are pregnant.' (1988:146) This combination of the physical and the cultural is intrinsic to Agar's overall view of her art.

2. In 1987 there was a retrospective of Agar's work at the Birch and Conran Gallery, London, which consolidated the growing appreciation of her contribution to twentieth-century art. See: Birch & Conran Fine Art, *Eileen Agar A Retrospective*, exhib. cat., text by Andrew Lambirth, 1987

3. *A Look at my Life* Eileen Agar 1988: 3

4. Leon Underwood's studio at Brook Green had a good reputation, especially for 'life drawing' and print techniques, and served Agar well as a basic introduction to her chosen profession. For an account of Underwood and his role as a teacher see: *Leon Underwood* by Christopher Neve.

5. Agar 1988: 73

6. Agar 1988: 84

7. The International Surrealist Exhibition was opened on 11 June 1936 by André Breton. It included about 390 paintings, sculptures, objects and drawings by artists from all over the world. The exhibition had been jointly organized by a British (Roland Penrose, Herbert Read, Paul Nash, Henry Moore and others) and a French committee formed by Breton, Paul Eluard, Man Ray and Georges Hugnet.

8. See pages 284-289 *Pablo Picasso: A retrospective* ed. William Rubin, Museum of Modern Art, New York, 1980.

9. Agar 1988: 84

10. Agar 1988: 112

11. The self-styled 'Comte de Lautréamont' or Isidore Ducasse (1846-1870) was an iconic figure for the surrealists, according to Breton 'For us there was no other genius who could stand comparison with Lautréamont'. His *Œvres Complètes* were published by the surrealist Georges Soupault in 1925.

12. Agar 1988: 112

13. Agar 1988: 115

14. André Breton *First Manifesto of Surrealism*, 1924 see: *Manifestoes of Surrealism*, trans. Richard Seaver & Helen R. Lane, Univ. of Michigan Press, Ann Arbor, 1969

15. Agar 1988:118

16. The horse head in QUADRIGA is based on a sculpted frieze from the Parthenon in Athens.

17. See: Whitney Chadwick *Women Artists and the Surrealist Movement*, Thames & Hudson, London, 1985

18. The original plaster head of *Angel of Anarchy* was a portrait of Bard, though various authors have suggested the title of the work is a reference to the anarchist politics of Herbert Read, see: 'Notes on Two Women Surrealist Painters' by Dawn Ades *Oxford Art Journal* 3 no. 1 April 1980

19. Agar 1988: 126

20. The 'Hat' was first exhibited in 1940 but has gone through various changes over the years, losing and aquiring decorative elements. In 1948 Agar appeared on British television modelling the hat for a show compèred by the costume historian James Laver. See: Agar 1988:168

21. Tenerife offered Agar and Bard a glimpse of pleasure and escape from the bleakness of post-war London and was according to Agar '...the islands of mystery and myth, the Fortunate Isles at the edge of the world...' (1988:181)

22. For a clear account of Abstract Expressionism see: Dore Ashton *The New York School*, New York, 1973.

23. This assertive masculinity was also recognized by the younger generation of artists associated with American Pop Art, such as Jasper Johns and Andy Warhol who found the aggresive intensity of artists like Pollock difficult to relate to, see: Andy Warhol *From A to B and back Again: The Philosophy of Andy Warhol*, Picador 1975

24. For a discussion of the position of women within Abstract Expressionism see: *Old Mistresss Women, Art and Ideology* by Rozika Parker & Griselda Pollock, 1981.

SELECT BIBLIOGRAPHY

INTRODUCTION

CHITTY, Susan *Gwen John*, London, Hodder & Stoughton 1981.

LANGDALE, Cecily & FRASER JENKINS, David *Gwen John An Interior Life*, Phaidon & Barbican Art Gallery 1985.

SONHAMI, Diana *Gluck, Her Biography*, London, Pandora 1988.

TAUBMAN, Mary *Gwen John* Scolar Press 1985.

SPALDING, Frances, *Vanessa Bell* London, Weidenfeld & Nicholson 1983.

CHAPTER ONE
LAURA KNIGHT

DUNBAR, Janet *Laura Knight* William Collins Sons & Co. Ltd. 1975.

FOX, Caroline *Dame Laura Knight* Oxford, Phaidon Press 1988.

(catalogue) *Painting in Newlyn 1900-1930* Penzance, Cornwall, Newlyn Orion 1985.

JAFFE, Patricia *Women Engravers*, London, Virago 1988.

KNIGHT, Laura *Oil Paint and Grease Paint* London, Ivor Nicholson & Watson 1936/Penguin Books 1941. *The Magic of a Line* London, William Kimber 1965.

A Proper Circus Omie London, Peter Davies 1962.

David Messum Gallery, (catalogue) *On With The Show* Drawings by Dame Laura Knight with a Foreword by Laura Wortley.

McCONKEY, Kenneth *British Impressionism* Oxford, Phaidon 1989.

See also: *Laura Knight: A Book of Drawings* (Limited Edition) with a Foreword by Charles Merriot, London, Bodley Head 1923.

Modern Masters of Etching: Laura Knight BBE,

ARA with an Introduction by Michael Saloman, London, The Studio 1932.

CHAPTER TWO
NINA HAMNETT

ANSCOME, Isabelle *Omega and After. Bloomsbury and the Decorative Arts*, London, Thames & Hudson 1981.

Anthony d'Offay Gallery (catalogue), *Omega Workshops – Alliance and Enmity in English Art 1911-1920*, London 1984.

BARON, Wendy *Sickert* Oxford, Phaidon 1973.

COLE, Roger *Burning to Speak: The Life and Art of Henri Gaudier-Brzeska* Oxford, Phaidon 1978.

COLLINS, Judith *The Omega Workshops*, London, Secker & Warburg 1984.

EDE, H.S. *Savage Messiah* London, Heinemann 1931.

FIFIELD, Williams *Modigliani. The Biography*

HAMNETT, Nina *Laughing Torso*, Constable London, 1932/Virago 1984.

Is She A Lady? A Problem in Autobiography London, Allan Wingate 1955.

HOLROYD, Michael *Augustus John* (in two vols.), London, Heinemann 1974 and 1975.

HOOKER, Denise *Nina Hamnett: Queen of Bohemia* London, Constable 1986.

JOHN, Augustus *Chiaroscuro* London, Cape 1952.

LESLIE, W. Seymour *The Silent Queen*, with illustrations by Nina Hamnett, London, Cape 1927.

SITWELL, Osbert *The People's Album of London Statues*, illustrated by Nina Hamnett, London, Duckworth 1928.

SPALDING, Frances *Roger Fry, Art and Life* London, Paul Elek/Granada 1980.

SUTTON, Denys *Letters of Roger Fry* (in two

vols.) London, Chatto and Windus 1972.

SYMONS, Julian *The Thirties* London, Cresset Press 1960.

CHAPTER THREE
CARRINGTON

BRENAN, Gerald *A Life of One's Own*, London, Hamish Hamilton 1962.

A Personal Record, London, Jonathan Cape 1974.

CARRINGTON, Noel *Carrington*, Oxford, Oxford Polytechnic Press 1978/USA Thames & Hudson 1980.

(Ed.) *Selected Letters of Mark Gertler*, Hart Davis 1965.

FIELDING, Xan *Best of Friends, The Brenan – Partridge Letters*, London, Chatto & Windus 1986.

GARNETT, David (Ed.) *Carrington, Letters and Extracts From Her Diaries*, Oxford University Press 1979.

GERZINA, Gretchen *Carrington, A Biography*, London, John Murray 1989.

HOLROYD, Michael *Lytton Strachey, A Biography*, London, Penguin Books 1971.

LEHMANN, Rosamond *Rosamond Lehmann's Albums*, London, Chatto & Windus.

MOSLEY, Diana *Loved Ones, Pen Portraits*, London, Sidgwick & Jackson 1985.

PARTRIDGE, Frances *Memories*, London, Victor Golancz 1981/Robin Clark 1982.

Friends in Focus, London, Chatto & Windus 1987.

STRACHEY, Julia & PARTRIDGE Frances *Julia, A Portrait of Julia Strachey*, London, Victor Golancz 1983/Penguin Books 1984.

WOODESON, John *Mark Gertler: Biography of a Painter 1891-1939*, Sidgwick & Jackson 1972.

SELECT BIBLIOGRAPHY

CHAPTER FOUR
WINIFRED NICHOLSON

COLLINS, Judith *Winifred Nicholson,* Tate
Gallery catalogue 1987.
LANE, John *The Living Tree: Art and the Sacred*
(Chapter on Winifred Nicholson), Green Books,
Bideford, Devon 1988.
NICHOLSON, Winifred *Paintings, Letters,*
Writings, An anthology compiled by Andrew
Nicholson, London, Faber and Faber 1987.
NICHOLSON, Winifred *Flower Tales,* (Limited
Edition) LYC Publications 1976.

CHAPTER FIVE
EILEEN AGAR

ADES, Dawn "Notes on Two Women Surrealist
Painters" in *Oxford Art Journal,* Vol. 111 no.
April 1980.
AGAR, Eileen *A Look at my Life,* with Andrew
Lambirth, Methuen, London, 1988.
CHADWICK, Whitney *Woman Artists and the*
Surrealist Movement, Thames & Hudson,
London 1985.
Commonwealth Art Gallery *Eileen Agar*
Retrospective exhib. cat., with an introduction by
Roland Penrose, London 1971.
Hayward Gallery, London *Dada and Surrealism*
Reviewed, exhib. cat., 1978.
New Burlington Gallery, *International Surrealist*
Exhibitions, cat. London 1936.
READ, Herbert *Surrealism,* Faber, London 1936.

The following is a mixed collection of books about women and art, feminist aesthetics, individual artists, and 20C British art. For material on the five artists in this book, see Select Bibliography.

ANSCOMBE, Isabelle *A Woman's Touch. Women in Design From 1860 to the Present,* London, Virago 1984.

BECKETT, Wendy *Contemporary Women Artists,* Oxford, Phaidon 1988.

BETTERTON, Rosemary *Looking On: Images of Femininity in the Visual Arts and Media,* London, Pandora 1987.

BROUDE, Norma & GARRARD, Mary D. (Eds.) *Feminism and Art History – Questioning the Litany.* New York, Harper & Row 1982.

CALLEN, Anthea *Angel in the Studio: Women in the Arts and Crafts Movement 1870-1914,* London, Astragal Books 1979.

CHERRY, Deborah (catalogue) *Painting Women: Victorian Women Artists,* Rochdale Art Gallery 1987.

COMPTON, Susan (Ed.) *British Art in the Twentieth Century,* Prestel Vergal & The Royal Academy of Arts London, 1986.

Crafts Council (catalogue) *The Omega Workshops – Decorative Arts of Bloomsbury,* London 1984.

ECKER, Gisela (Ed.) *Feminist Aesthetics,* London, Women's Press 1985.

GARB, T. *Women Impressionists,* Oxford, Phaidon 1986.

GERRISH NUNN, Pamela (Ed.) *Canvassing – Recollections by Six Victorian Women Artists,* London, Camden Press 1986.

Victorian Women Artists, London, The Women's Press 1987.

GREER, Germaine *The Obstacle Race,* London, Secker & Warburg 1979/Picador 1981.

HELLER, Nancy G. *Women Artists An Illustrated History,* New York, Abbeville/London, Virago 1987.

HIGNETT, Sean *Brett, From Bloomsbury to New Mexico* London, Hodder & Stoughton 1984.

HESS, Thomas B. & BAKER, Elizabeth (Eds.) *Art and Sexual Politics,* London, Collier Macmillan 1973.

KENT, Sarah and Mirreau Jaccqueline (Eds.) *Women's Images of Men,* London, Writers and Readers 1985.

KRUGER, Barbara (catalogue) *We Won't Play Nature to your Culture,* text by Craig Owens & Jane Weinstock, London ICA 1983.

KRULL, Edith *Women in Art,* Studio Vista 1986.

KUHN, Annette *The Power of the Image: Essays on Representation and Sexuality,* Routledge & Kegan, London 1985.

LANGDALE, Cecily & FRASER JENKINS, David *Gwen John An Interior Life,* Phaidon & Barbican Art Gallery 1985.

LIPPARD, Lucy *From the Center: Feminist essays on Women's Art,* New York 1976.

LINKER. K. *Difference: On Representation and Sexuality,* New York, New Museum of Contemporary Art 1985.

MARSH, J. *The Pre-Raphaelite Sisterhood,* London, Quartet Books 1985.

MORRIS, Meaghan *The Pirate's Fiancée,* London, Verso 1988.

MULVEY, Laura *Visual and Other Pleasures,* London, Macmillan 1989.

NOCHLIN, L. and SUTHERLAND HARRIS, A. *Women Artists 1550-1990,* New York, Alfred Knopf 1976.

NOCHLIN, Linda *Women, Art and Power and Other Essays* New York 1988.

Nottingham Castle Museum, (catalogue) *Women's Art Show 1550-1970,* Nottingham 1982.

OWESU, Kwesi (Ed.) *Storms of the Heart – An Anthology of Black Women's Culture,* Camden Press 1988.

PARKER, R. and POLLOCK, G. *Old Mistresses: Women Art and Ideology,* London, Routledge & Kegan 1981/Pandora 1986.

Framing Feminism: Art and the Women's Movement 1979-85, London, Pandora 1987.

PETERSON, Karen & WILSON, J.J. *Women Artists,* London, The Women's Press 1987.

POLLOCK, Griselda *Vision and Difference, Femininity, Feminism and the Histories of Art,* London/New York, Routledge 1988.

Mary Cassatt London, Jupiter Books 1980.

ROBINSON, Hilary (Ed.) *Feminism and Art Today, An Anthology,* London, Camden Press 1987.

SAUNDERS, Lesley (Ed.) *Glancing Fires – An Investigation Into Women's Creativity,* London, Women's Press 1987.

SELLARS, Jane (catalogue) *Women's Works,* National Museums and Galleries on Merseyside 1988.

SHONE, Richard *A Century of Change: British Painting since 1990,* Oxford 1977.

Bloomsbury Portraits, Oxford, Phaidon 1976.

SPALDING, Hilary *British Art Since 1900,* London, Thames & Hudson 1986.

STREIER RUBINSTEIN, Charlotte *American Women Artists,* Avon Books 1982.

TICKNER, Lisa *The Spectacle of Women – Imagery of the Suffrage Campaign 1907-14,* Chatto & Windus 1987.

WARNER, Marina *Alone of All Her Sex,* Weidenfeld & Nicholson 1976.

Monuments and Maidens: The Allegory of the Female Form, London 1985.

WATNEY, Simon *English Post-Impressionism,* London, Studio Vista 1980.

WILLIAMS, Val *Women Photographers,* Virago 1986.

Women Artists Slide Library *Eye to Eye: Irish Women Artists,* London 1986.
Women's Work: Two Years in the Life of a Women Artist's Group, London, Brixton Art Gallery 1986.

Titles of paintings are in small capitals;
titles of books in italic. Page numbers in
italic refer to illustrations.

A

Abstract Expressionists 179-80
ACCORD (Nicholson) 149-52
Action Painting 180
Agar, Eileen 10, 15, 22, 25, 161-80, *163, 171*
ALLEZ-OOP (Knight) 39, *42*
Allied Artists Association 11-12, 76
ANGEL OF ANARCHY (Agar) *158,* 172-4, *173*
ANNIE (Carrington) 108
ASSISTANT SECTION LEADER E HENDERSON,
    MM AND SERGEANT D TURNER MM
    (Knight) 44
AT THE CAR DOOR (Knight) 40
AUTOBIOGRAPHY OF AN EMBRYO (Agar) *156,*
    166, 169
automatic painting 179

B

ballet paintings (Laura Knight) 33-8
BALLOON SITE, COVENTRY, A (Knight) 44,
    45
BANK HOLIDAY (Knight) *34,* 38
Bard, Joseph 162, *165,* 174, 175
Barron, Phyllis 19
Bartlett, Robin 162
BATTLE CRY, BULLET PROOF PAINTING (Agar)
    174-5, *177*
BEACH, THE (Knight) 30, *31*
Bell, Clive 13, 17
Bell, Vanessa 10, 12-13, 15, 16, 17, 18, 61,
    62, 98, 103
BEN WITH JAKE (Nicholson) *125,* 127
Bevan, Robert 12
Bewick, Mary 149, 150
Bloomsbury Group 13, 83, 110, 111, 112
BLUE HEPTAGONS (Nicholson) *134,* 144, 146
Bomberg, David 86
book illustrations 19-20
Borenius, Tancred 76
Bowen, Stella 112

BOY WITH CONCERTINA (Carrington) 108,
    109
BOYS, THE (Knight) 30
Braden, Nora 19
Brenan, Gerald 86, 88, 98, 112
Breton, André 161, 166, 167, 169, 172
Brett, Dorothy 15, 87
Brzeska, Sophie 66, 67
Bunting, Basil 70-1, 76
Byam Shaw, John 122

C

CACTUS (Carrington) *107,* 108
Camden Town Group 12, 62
CANDLEMASS I (Nicholson) 127
Carrington, Catharine *85,* 108
Carrington, Dora 9, 15, 16, 18, 22, 47, *82,*
    83-116, 161
CATHARINE CARRINGTON (Carrington) *85,*
    108
CEREMONIAL HAT FOR EATING
    BOUILLABAISSE (Agar) *158,* 175, *177*
Cézanne, Paul 21, 61, 62, 123
CHARIVARI (Knight) 39, *46*
China, women court artists in 142
circus paintings (Laura Knight) 38-40
Colefax, Sybil, Lady 18
COLLIURE (Hamnett) 62, *81*
COMPANIONS (Nicholson) 149-52
Contemporary Art Society 148
COPPER AND CAPARI (Nicholson) *136,* 140-2
Costa, Giovanni 122
craft galleries 19
Crowley, Aleister 78
Cumberland Market Group 12
Cunard, Emerald, Lady 18
CYCLAMEN AND PRIMULA (Nicholson) *138*

D

Dacre, Isabel 12
Dali, Salvador *171,* 175, 179
DAWN AND THE GOLDEN GIRL (Knight) 30-2
DELUGE, THE (Knights) *14*
DOCK, NUREMBERG, THE (Knight) 46
DOLORES (Hamnett) *73,* 74, *90*
Drawn From Life (Bowen) 112

DRESSING ROOM AT DRURY LANE, A
    (Knight) *36,* 37
DRESSING THE CHILDREN (Knight) 28

E

Ede, Jim 147
ELDER SISTER, THE (Knight) 28
Eluard, Paul 161, 166, *171,* 174
Epstein, Jacob 67
Etchells, Jessie 12, 13
Etruscan School 122
Euston Road School of Painters 12
exhibitions by women painters 11-13

F

FEET BATHING PARTY, THE (Carrington) *115*
FIRE AND WATER (Nicholson) *124,* 125
Fisher Prout, Margaret 10, 15-16, *17*
flower painting 21-2; *see also* Nicholson,
    Winifred
Flower Tales (Nicholson) 122
FLYING A KITE (Knight) 30
Forbes, Stanhope 29
Friday Club 12, 13
Fry, Roger 11, 13, 18, 21-2, 59, 74, 76, 88,
    99
    and Nina Hamnett 58, 60-1, 62, *63,* 64,
    71, 72, 77

G

galleries 19
GATE TO THE ISLES, THE (Nicholson) *151*
Gaudier-Brzeska, Henri 63, 66-7, *68,* 71
GAUDY BEGGARS (Knight) 40
GENTLEMAN WITH A TOP HAT (Hamnett)
    74, *91*
Gertler, Mark 18, 86, 87, 88, *97*
GILES LYTTON STRACHEY (Carrington) *95,*
    108, 110
Gill, Winifred 64
Gilman, Harold 62
Glasgow Society of Lady Artists 12
Gluck (Hannah Gluckstein) *14,* 16
GOBLET AND TWO PEARS (Ben Nicholson)
    128
Gosse, Sylvia 10, 12, 16
Grant, Duncan 13, 16, 18, 61, 62, 98, 103

Greenaway, Kate 19

H

Hamilton, Lady Ian, Countess of Drogheda
    18
Hamnett, Nina 9-10, 12, 22, 57-80, *59*, 86,
    110, 161
Hassall, Joan 20
HAY MAKING (Carrington) 98
HEPBURN, JAMES (Hamnett) *72*, 93
Hepworth, Barbara 17, 120, 143, 149
Herkomer, Hubert von 15
Hermes, Gertrude 20
Hiles, Barbara 87
HILLS IN THE SNOW AT HURSTBOURNE
    TARRANT (Carrington) 87, *97*
Hodgkins, Frances 10, 18-19
Holroyd, Michael 78
Hone, Evie 16
HONEYSUCKLE AND SWEETPEAS (Nicholson)
    135, 142
Hooker, Denise 78
Howard, Rosalind, Countess of Carlisle
    121
Hudson, Anna 16
Hutton, Dorothy 19
Hynes, Sheila 77

I

IN FOR REPAIRS (Knight) 41-4
Is She A Lady? (Hamnett) 58, 76, 78
ISLE OF CANNA (Nicholson) 140, *141*

J

JAKE AND KATE ON THE ISLE OF WIGHT
    (Nicholson) *125*, 127, 143
Jellet, Mainie 16
John, Augustus 11, 17, 18, 40-1, 60, 67, 110
    and Nina Hamnett 75, 76, 77-8, 79
John, Gwen 10, 14, 15, 17, 18, 104, 110
Johnson, Charlotte 26
JULIA STRACHEY (Carrington) 108

K

Karlowska, Stanislawa de 12
Kemp-Welch, Lucy 15
Knight, Dame Laura 9, 17, 22, 23-48, *24*,

36, *43*, 75, 77, 161
Knight, Harold 9, 17, 27, 28, 29, 48
Knights, Winifred 10, 14, 15, 17
KNITTING LESSON, THE (Knight) 28
Kramer, Jacob 76
Kristian, Roald 63, 68-70
Kuhlenthal, Christine 87

L

LAMORNA COVE (Knight) 32
LANDLADY, THE (Hamnett) 62, *69*, 72
LANDSCAPE IN PROVENCE (Hamnett) 62, *81*
Lane, Constance 87
Larcher, Dorothy 19
LARREAU SNOWSCAPE (Carrington) *115*
Laughing Torso (Hamnett) 58, 67, 68, 70,
    76, 78, 80
Leighton, Clare 20
Lewis, Wyndham 18
Li Yuan Chia 147
Little Gallery 19
LIVE PEWTER (Nicholson) 137, *139*
LOOKING IN THE GLASS (Knight) *34*
Lopokova, Lydia 33, 38

M

Magic of a Line, The (Knight) 25, 39, 46
Mairet, Ethel 19
MAJOR GENERAL BETHUNE LINDSAY
    (Hamnett) *73*, 75
MALE NUDE (Hamnett) *65*, 67
Manchester Society of Women Painters 12
MARCH MANY WEATHERS (Knight) 30
Marigold Garden, The (Greenaway) 19
MARINE OBJECT (Agar) 174, *176*
Marriott, Charles 74
Masson, André 169, 179
Medici Society 20
MILL AT TIDMARSH, BERKSHIRE, THE
    (Carrington) 87, 88, *96*
MODERN MUSE, THE (Agar) *155*, 167, 168
Modigliani, Amedeo 67-8, 71, 72
MOONLIGHT, POTS LOAN (Nicholson) 137
Morrell, Lady Ottoline 18
Mosley, Diana 102-3

MOTHER AND CHILD (Knight) 28
MOUNTAIN RANGES FROM YEGEN,
    ANDALUSIA (Carrington) 87, *130*
MOVEMENT IN SPACE (Agar) *164*, 166
MRS BOX (Carrington) 108-10, *109*
MRS CAMPBELL'S ROOM OF 1951 (Nicholson)
    146-7
MUGHETTI (Nicholson) *133*, 140, 142

N

Naper, Ella 32
Nash, John 87, 98
Nash, Paul 44, 86, 87, 98, 167, 168
Neve, Christopher 137, 146
Nevinson, Christopher 86
New English Art Club 11, 76
New Handworkers Gallery 19
Newlyn School 29-30
Nicholson, Ben 9, 17, *119*, 120, 123, 126,
    127, 143, 144, 146, 147, 148, 149
Nicholson, Winifred 9, 16, 17, 22, 25, 117-
    52, *118*, *119*, 161
NIGHT AND DAY (Nicholson) *150*
Nochlin, Linda 20-1
Norsworthy, Gwendoline 19

O

Oilpaint and Greasepaint (Knight) 25, 37,
    40
Omega Workshops 13, 18, 63, 64, 99, 102
ON THE CLIFFS (Knight) 32
Orpen, Sir William 11, 60
OSSIP ZADKINE (Hamnett) 74, *89*
OUTWARD (Nicholson) 146

P

PANDORA'S BOX (Carrington) *101*, 102
PARIS LIGHT (Nicholson) 143, *145*
Paris Salon 12
Partridge, Frances 112
Partridge, Ralph 86, 112
Pavlova, Anna 38
Penrose, Alec and Frances 103
Penrose, Roland 168, *171*, 174
PENZANCE FAIR (Knight) *35*, 38
Picasso, Pablo 47, 57, 61, 62, 68, 99, 167,

INDEX

PICKING VEGETABLES (Carrington) 98
Pleydell Bouverie, Katherine 19
Pollock, Jackson 179
POLYANTHUS AND CINERARIA (Nicholson) 138, 140
Post-Impressionism 13, 61
Potter, Beatrix 19-20
Pound, Ezra 66, 166
PRISMATIC FIVE (Nicholson) 152, 154
Proctor, Dod 10, 17, 29
Proper Circus Omnie, A (Knight) 39

Q

QUADRIGA (Agar) 157, 169, 174
Quinn, John 18

R

Raine, Kathleen 140, 147, 148
RAPE OF THE SABINE WOMEN, THE (Waugh) 15
Raverat, Gwen 20
ROCKS AT PLOUMANACH, BRITTANY (Agar) 175, 178
ROMANIES AT EPSOM (Knight) 40
Rooke, Noel 20
Rose, Muriel 19
Rothenstein, William 88
Royal Academy Schools 13-15
RUBY LOFTUS SCREWING A BREECH-RING (Knight) 40, 44
RUPERT DOONE (Hamnett) 72, 92, 93
Rutter, Frank 127
Ryland, Dr George 101, 104

S

Sadler, Sir Michael 76
Sands, Ethel 16
SEASHORE MONSTER, THE (Agar) 168, 170
SELF-PORTRAIT WITH NUDE (Knight) 32
SHEEP SHEARING (Carrington) 98
Sickert, Walter 11, 12, 16, 21, 22, 58, 60, 61, 64, 66, 70, 71, 72
Sitwell, Osbert 64, 67, 71
Slade School of Fine Art 13, 15
Smith, Matthew 76
Society of Women Artists 12

Spencer, Stanley 86, 87
STILL LIFE NO.1 (Hamnett) 62
Strachey, Alix 105, 108, 110, 113, 114
Strachey, Julia 108, 116
Strachey, Lytton 9, 16, 71, 83, 84, 85, 88, 102, 103, 104, 105, 111-12, 113-14
portraits of 95, 108, 110
STURM, DER (Hamnett) 62, 89
SUMMERTIME, CORNWALL (Knight) 32, 51
Surrealism
and Eileen Agar 10, 161, 166-7, 168-75
Sutherland, Graham 44, 46
Swynnerton, Annie 12

T

TAKE OFF (Knight) 41
Tarrant, Margaret 19, 20
TELL YOUR FORTUNE, LADY (Knight) 40
THREE CLOWNS (Knight) 39
THREE FIGURES IN A CAFE (Hamnett) 69
Three Shields Gallery 19
Twenties Group 19
TWO GIRLS ON A CLIFF (Knight) 31, 32

U

Underwood, Leon 161, 162
Unknown Colour (Nicholson) 120
Unwin, George Manuel 74-5

V

Van Gogh, Vincent 21, 22, 72, 99
VILLA CARPRICCIO, LUGANO (Jake Nicholson) 124
Vision and Design (Fry) 21

W

Wadsworth, Edward 76
Walden, Herwath 62
Waley, Margaret 102
Walker, Ethel 15
Waugh, Edna (later Lady Clarke Hall) 15
Weight, Carel 16
Wertheim, Lucy 19
Wickham, Anna 72
WINDOW-SILL, LUGANO (Nicholson) 148
WOMAN ROCKING A CRADLE (Van Gogh) 72
Women's International Arts Club 12

wood engravers 20
Woolf, Virginia 11, 12, 13, 15, 102, 111

Y

YOUNG WOMAN HOLDING A BLACK CAT (Gwen John) 14

Z

Zawadowski, Waclow 70